CULTURE IS THE NEW LEADERSHIP

WHAT EVERY LEADER NEEDS TO KNOW ABOUT ENGAGEMENT, PERFORMANCE, AND ORGANIZATIONAL EFFECTIVENESS

CULTURE IS THE NEW LEADERSHIP

WHAT EVERY LEADER
NEEDS TO KNOW ABOUT
ENGAGEMENT, PERFORMANCE,
AND ORGANIZATIONAL
EFFECTIVENESS

BY BENJAMIN ORTLIP

IVY LEAGUE PRESS

Copyright © 2024 by Benjamin Ortlip

All rights reserved

No portion of this book may be reproduced, stored in a retrieval system, or transmitted in any form by any means–electronic, mechanical, photocopy, recording, or other–except for brief quotations in printed reviews, without prior permission of the author.

Hardcover: 979-8-9907340-0-5
Paperback: 979-8-9907340-1-2
eBook: 979-8-9907340-2-9

This book is dedicated to Ray Willoch,

a model American businessman,

and the consummate father-in-law.

ACKNOWLEDGEMENTS

Lisa, my wife and business partner: your wisdom is more precious than gold.

Drew Kaiser: you make everything you do look easy, and everything I do seem fun.

Bob Keator and David Watters: thanks for your ability to take vision and make reality.

Phil Orazi, Mark Miller, Ken Blanchard, Henry Cloud, John Maxwell: you taught me everything I know about leadership.

Rick Wartzman, Peter Drucker: you taught me everything I know about management.

Jeff Gray: you taught me tons of other stuff.

Zach, Tony, Blake, Robert, David, Bobby: you were the real visionaries.

Brent Cole, Gabe Lyons, Jason Locy, Tim Willard, Chris Arias: you taught me how to write.

Steve Beecham, Lisa McGuire, Chuck Allen, Rilla Delorier, Jonathan McCoy, Erik Løkkesmoe: you encouraged me.

Peggy Pullen: you taught me to type properly — not a day goes by without my gratitude for this gift!

CONTENTS

PROLOGUE Maslow Was Right XI

CHAPTER 1 The Problem With People 1

CHAPTER 2 Igniting Culture 19

CHAPTER 3 A Brief History of Work 29

CHAPTER 4 Culture Happens 42

CHAPTER 5 M1: Safety 63

CHAPTER 6 M2: Compensation 73

CHAPTER 7 M3: Efficiency 81

CHAPTER 8 M4: Training 87

CHAPTER 9 M5: Workload 92

CHAPTER 10 M6: Stress Level 97

CHAPTER 11 M7: Job-fit 102

CHAPTER 12 L1: Vision 112

CHAPTER 13 L2: Advancement 124

CHAPTER 14 L3: Innovation 129

CHAPTER 15 L4: Empathy 138

CHAPTER 16 L5: Clout. 143

CHAPTER 17 C1: Craft 158

CHAPTER 18 C2: Cause 173

CHAPTER 19 C3: Community 181

EPILOGUE   A Message For The C-Suite. 190

PROLOGUE

MASLOW WAS RIGHT

"What a man can be, he must be. We call this need self-actualization."

~ Abraham Maslow

If you don't make it any further in this book, let this one thought sink in:

> For the first time in the history of the world, the workforce has reached what Abraham Maslow called "self-actualization."

I know, it's a bit of a mouthful.

But that one statement contains the most significant development in the business landscape today. It's at the root of everything. In that one statement are the answers to the very challenges that confound today's leaders.

What issues do you see when you look around? Is rapid change overwhelming daily operations? Is the shift to remote work disrupting progress? Do you see increased difficulties with recruiting and retention? Employee burnout? How about all of the above?

There's a golden thread running through all the common maladies of today's workplace. And if you follow that thread to the end, it leads to a major shift in the role that work plays in civilization itself:

> *Work is no longer just a means to an end. It is now an end unto itself.*

It's a human reality that when a job fails to meet key psychological needs, a person's sense of drive shuts down. Multiply this phenomenon across the company and you've got a serious problem on your hands. Multiply it across 3.4 billion people, and you've got today's global workforce – discontented, disconnected, and disengaged.

There's a fundamental shift behind this worldwide phenomenon. That's what this book is about.

This is not the first book about company culture. To date, the Library of Congress recognizes 437 volumes that actually contain the word "culture" in the title, and hundreds more that deal with the topic at some level. We don't need another book that merely chips away at the psychological mysteries that throttle human performance.

It's time to put the pieces together.

When the mountain puffs smoke at increasing intervals, an eruption is imminent.

Across the modern workplace, molten lava has been oozing for more than three decades, burning through desperate management efforts as it rolls downhill. It's not that we've failed to detect any seismic activity, but we've yet to call it what it really is: a human resource earthquake… a silent humanitarian crisis. The cost it brings in terms of turnover and disengagement is massive. The average organization is losing 31% of what it spends on payroll every single year! That's the equivalent of a car that gets 8 miles per gallon. It might be an acceptable way to cruise the strip, but it's no way to run a company.

My work puts me face to face with the rank-and-file sufferers who often burst into tears when given the invitation to tell me where it hurts. Let's not even address the mental health burdens created by the noxious environment of a thoughtless culture.

When a workforce reaches self-actualization the differences can be subtle, but the implications reach across global economies and penetrate down to the neural pathways where things like ambition and commitment and concentration are decided.

Maslow described this entire phenomenon nearly a century ago.

Maslow, as you may recall, was the psychologist who observed that our motivations in life are entirely dependent on our station in life. Basically, hungry people yearn for food, fed people yearn for meaning, and so on.

As a global workforce, we've been climbing slowly up Maslow's famous hierarchy of needs since the beginning of civilization. The vast majority of human effort throughout that time has been fueled by basic survival needs: food, shelter, clothing, etc. However, the past century has seen monumental changes. Today's workers are much more evolved, and that makes today's workplace much more complex. How do you motivate people to perform basic tasks inside an organization when the true hunger in their soul is to experience social connection, or to build better mousetraps, or to change the world? How do you connect those dots so the organization can keep churning forward?

These are the questions upon which the future of the workplace pivots. Those who discover the answers and solve the riddles will build kingdoms. Those who don't will perish, abandoned by a workforce that has moved on.

For the past fifty years or so, the success of most organizations has been determined by strategies that fall under a category called *leadership*. The emergence of leadership as a skillset has enabled more growth - and more *accelerated* growth - than at any other time in history.

When it first rose to prominence in business conversations, the concept of leadership was actually a little fuzzy. Discussions about it mostly emphasized the idea of having a personality and a presence that others found inspiring. Leadership meant a natural instinct for taking charge. It meant the ability to form connections with workers at all levels, and even to groom them to move into leadership roles themselves. Leadership was something everyone recognized but few could explain very well.

As an organizational discipline, leadership wasn't a codified subject... yet.

By the end of the 20th century, leadership had become one of the most proliferated topics in business. Leadership books had earned their own section in bookstores. There were leadership models, leadership seminars... coaches, workshops, academic majors, and entire institutes dedicated to advancing its pillars.

The key thing to note about leadership is that it wasn't *invented* in the 20th century, but that it was finally *codified* during that period. In fact, it was the achievement of codifying leadership that enabled companies to replicate leadership practices and drive an explosion of business growth.

Generally speaking, *culture* - the organizational discipline of fostering an engaged, productive workforce - is where *leadership* was about a century ago. Today, culture is something everyone recognizes but few can explain very well. Like leadership, culture has always been there. But it will be the ability to *codify* culture as an organizational discipline that enables companies - and people like you - to harness it for the next wave of explosive economic growth. It's already beginning to happen in many places. Books have been written to highlight various components of culture. Tools have been introduced to collect employee feedback. New platforms aim to foster community in the face of hybrid work models and virtual meeting environments.

Identifying the components and tools is a great start, but the achievement that qualifies any skillset as an institutional discipline - whether it's management, leadership, or culture - is the ability to quantify it… to recognize what it is, and what it isn't… to identify all the factors that influence it… then to measure and manage those factors. To codify it.

That's what this book is about.

Culture is no longer a nebulous concept or an elusive "vibe" — it's a new operational discipline that all great organizations manage with scrutiny and vigilance. Culture is the new leadership!

QUITTING IS STARTING IN DISGUISE

In the 1980s, I had a dream job in the advertising industry writing commercials and promoting a number of household brands. I got to work with famous athletes and entertainers. My clients were some of the world's top companies. The pay was good. The hours were reasonable. And the future glowed with potential.

There was just one problem: I was *miserable*.

I couldn't put my finger on it at the time. How could such a great job be simultaneously so bad? I was conflicted.

My Judeo-Christian upbringing had plenty to say about work ethic. And yet I felt increasingly powerless to resist the malaise that overcame me. On the outside, I was going through the motions just fine. On the inside, I was slowly dying. At first I tried to fight it. Then to hide it.

Ultimately I decided it was best to be honest about it… at least with myself. So I stopped trying to hide it and I just let it play out in the open. I knew there would be consequences, but I couldn't bear the thought of spending the rest of my career in silent misery. Whatever was wrong with me, I wasn't willing to go on. At one point I even began documenting my symptoms on a conference room wall for all to see. It was a scene straight out of *Jerry Maguire*. Eventually, in an effort to expose my disintegrating value to the company, I simply stopped coming to work. I wasn't really showing up in spirit, so why pretend otherwise? I checked myself out voluntarily. Thirty years before the Great Resignation of 2021, I staged my own personal walk-out.

At the time, it was confusing. I had no global pandemic to blame. There were no articles in Forbes about all the other people quitting their jobs. I wasn't part of a workplace revolution. There was nothing triumphant about it. I simply felt like I didn't measure up… that I lacked the discipline to fit the world's system.

Little did I know, I wasn't alone. At the exact same time my career was hitting the reset button, millions of workers around the world were also turning up infected with the same strange symptoms. The outbreak was so significant that in 1990, the Gallup organization launched a global assessment to study this bizarre phenomenon. They termed the condition *disengagement*. For more than three decades since, Gallup has been tracking the progression of this syndrome across the workplace in its now-famous Q12 study.

As it turns out, by facing my condition directly and honestly, I'd managed to escape.

In a twist of fate, I was recruited to write and consult on the very principles that had been shaping my workplace experience from the beginning. I worked alongside some of the most prominent thought-leaders and authors in the areas of management and leadership. I learned their ideas inside-out as a ghostwriter, a consultant, and a content creator. In the process, I was being taught about the inner workings of employee motivation. I came face-to-face with the dynamics that determine the difference between career misery and career fulfillment. I came to understand how management, leadership, and culture impact worker motivation and performance. I discovered why my dream job in advertising had ended in disappointment.

Most importantly, I recognized a monumental development - an inflection point - in the nature of work itself. It's a change so significant that it will topple global brands on its way to altering the way people work for the foreseeable future.

In short, the next half-century of work hinges on the ability of organizations to codify culture. As I'll share, that's precisely what I've been doing for the past three decades. Along the way, I've been implementing these concepts inside some of the greatest companies in business today. And just like I've been doing for leaders in a wide variety of industries, I'm going to tell you precisely what you need to be doing, how much of it you need to be doing, and what you should expect as a result of doing it.

CHICKEN SOUP FOR THE WORKFORCE

In 2011, the executive team at Zaxby's asked for help with their culture. When it was founded in 1987, Zaxby's had been an instant hit across the Southeast. It served chicken with an unmistakable swagger. Zaxby's was like Chick-Fil-A's cooler, younger brother. For its founders, Zach and Tony, the company was an extension of their childhood friendship, and included a vast network of friends and business colleagues. But, twenty years later, the brand had hit a wall. Their franchisees were complacent. The whole brand was listless.

I was invited to work closely with the C-suite to implement the same principles I'll share in this book. In just three years, Zaxby's doubled its revenue without significant personnel changes. Simply put, the brand turned up the engagement of its existing people. Soon after, the company was acquired by Goldman-Sachs in a lucrative deal.

That's the impact of codifying culture.

Zaxby's is just one of many examples. The same scenario has played out in numerous restaurant chains, in healthcare, in manufacturing, in telecommunications, and in transportation. In company after company, these same concepts have been unlocking the reserves that are pent up in the workforce today. And they can work for you too.

All businesses stand on the same three legs: product, process, and people. The product leg represents the goods or services you bring to market. The process leg refers to the systems used to deliver them profitably. And the people leg stands for the wide variety of human efforts along the way. Here's the important thing to notice: since the Industrial Revolution, extensive work has been done to maximize the value and efficiency of product development. Likewise, we've squeezed every ounce of incremental gain from process improvement. Products and processes have been examined, codified, and streamlined ad nauseam. However, the people leg – the science of human performance – has remained a bit of a mystery.

We've been skipping leg day!

Casual Fridays, ping-pong tables, and attaboys don't even scratch the surface of the sophisticated science begging to be exploited. They're as laughable as a Dundie Award. The people leg is a blue ocean, waiting to be harnessed for the next wave of economic growth.

MORE THAN A FEELING

The problem with most conversations about culture is that they focus on the feelings of their people. Employee feelings have their place, but in order to affect engagement and effort, you have to go one level deeper to employee needs. Needs govern the subconscious allocation of effort. When you understand how to operate at the level of employee need, it's like strapping yourself into the cockpit of a powerful new machine.

The problem with feelings is that most jobs are just that: a job. Needs, however, represent a door to a person's core motivations. As you'll soon see, there's a glitch in the employer-employee matrix that applies to all work everywhere, whether you're curing cancer or licking envelopes in a dimly-lit supply room. The glitch was the key to doubling revenue at Zaxby's. The glitch is your yacht for navigating the blue ocean of people… steroids for the people leg of the business.

The principles I'm about to share have unleashed billions of dollars in incremental productivity and profitability for big and small companies alike, in a wide variety of industries – most of it coming from front-line workers performing the most menial of jobs. The key lies in taking proper inventory of the many diverse motivations (and the deterrents) that influence how every individual approaches their work.

Reflect:
Have you noticed a change in the mentality toward work?

CHAPTER 1

THE PROBLEM WITH PEOPLE

"I find it enjoyable to think about business or investment problems. They're easy. It's the human problems that are the tough ones. Sometimes there aren't any good answers with human problems."

~ Warren Buffett

Everywhere you look, people are operating at a fraction of their potential. They're talented. They're trained. They're empowered. They might even be highly motivated. But somehow they're always leaving something on the table. If your professional success depends on the performance of others, you know exactly what I'm talking about. Your job is a never-ending sequence of problem-solving exercises aimed at getting your people to produce the needed results. It could be a familiar problem that seems to raise its head over and over again. Or maybe it's something new and unpredictable that requires an out-of-the-box solution. In either case the result is the same: performance falls short of expectations.

When I say performance I'm not talking about the difference between, say, the current world record for running a mile and the one to be set by some super-athlete from the future. I'm talking about the way everyday humans *perform* everyday tasks, every single day. Take the speed at which you're reading this, for example. Or the comprehension. No doubt you're capable of reading faster when you want to. You know how to be more focused and efficient when the situation calls for it. And yet you've settled on this way of reading instead. Why is that? It's not like it doesn't add up over the course of your life, affecting the number of books you read and the information you retain. The same thing is true when workers settle into their pace of performance on the job. It adds up over time and can mean millions of dollars in fluctuating output for the company.

Yes, there's something inherently *human* about human performance. It doesn't conform to the modern business ethos which runs on big data, process automation, and predictive analytics. While leaders feel a greater sense of control from the algorithms that guide businesses today, the science of human performance seems stuck. The vast majority of workers are disengaged. It's been this way for more than thirty years, and other than measuring this horrifying statistic no one seems to know what to do about it. The more advanced we become at mastering all the other business operations, the more difficult it becomes to paint over the enigma of human behavior as a central function of business. When people perform, it's invaluable. And when they don't, it's paralyzing. Workflows get backed up. Critical timings become disrupted. And core strategies are rendered impotent.

Here's what it looks like in the real world: a team of sales associates that's perfectly capable of producing $100,000 a month is stuck at $79,000 instead. Airline gate agents who should be turning 90% on-time departures are struggling to climb above 65%. Restaurant franchises designed to average $3M in annual revenue are only doing $1.9M. Sales associates are missing quotas. Line workers are turning out defects. On and on it goes. People who are perfectly capable of performing at one level are continually coming up short of their potential. Well short.

This is especially concerning when it's your job to generate performance. It might remind you of that classic vaudeville act with the spinning plates. The entertainer balances several spinning plates on a row of sticks; as soon as he gets the last one spinning strong, the first one starts to wobble. You find yourself running back and forth across the organization keeping things spinning so the act can continue. Sometimes the problem is an operational issue. Other times it's training. Or equipment. Or competitors. Or the economy. There are all kinds of factors that cause the plates to wobble. And it's your job to make sure the show goes on.

Allow me to suggest a simpler view of things. As complex as your world may be — and I don't doubt that it is — things get a lot clearer when you start to view them as one single issue: **culture.**

So how can I justify such an apparent oversimplification? After all, the term *culture* has tribal connotations. Culture refers to people. Culture is not the company, it's merely the layer of humanity that spreads itself across a company. Culture refers to the teams that operate in and around the machinery. It's the artifacts that mark their presence. Culture means the leaders who decide when the doors will open and close. That's culture, right?

A century ago, human behavior and performance were thought of as separate from the machinery of the organization itself. The machinery — that monolithic assemblage of industrial muscle that churned out products and supported families — was the centerpiece. Sure, people worked in the buildings and operated the equipment. But their individual personalities and work styles and human-ness were tangential. On Henry Ford's assembly line, for example, people were more like flesh-and-bone robots, needed mainly for their basic ability to memorize a routine and perform it over and over. The rest of their humanity — such as the ability to reason, to make moral judgments, to feel emotion, to bond with others, etc. — was actually a liability that had to be managed out of the equation. Workers whose human qualities could not be compartmentalized adequately were simply replaced.

Traditionally, therefore, the term *culture* has referred to those designated places within an organization where human-ness was either embraced or, in most cases, merely tolerated. In particular, it was embraced in the boardrooms where core values needed to be crystallized, and it was tolerated in the break rooms where camaraderie had a useful therapeutic effect that helped workers to endure their robotic existence. Culture was separate from "real business" — things like strategy, and operations, and finance. Bring up culture in those conversations and you were likely to get a sideways glance.

Today, however, the topic of culture is routinely included in high-level conversations. But are we kidding ourselves to talk strategically about a topic that most leaders struggle to define clearly?

From Machinery To People

In 1967, three astronauts were burned alive during a test of the Apollo 1 spacecraft. It was a defining moment for NASA, the agency charged with carrying out President Kennedy's vision of landing a man on the moon by the end of the decade. The language that emerged in the wake of the disaster is telltale. In the investigative report that followed there was no mention of culture. There were no conversations about human failure or culpability. Instead, they seemed to regard it as a problem with the inanimate inner workings of industry and science. Here's an excerpt:

> "The Board's investigation revealed many deficiencies in design and engineering, manufacture and quality control. When these deficiencies are corrected the overall reliability of the Apollo Program will be increased greatly."

In other words, the machinery was wrong. Human error didn't become the focus of causality because human error was to be expected. Human error wasn't something you resolved through any business disciplines that existed at the time. The answer to the organization's problems, they reasoned, would be found in the machinery at the center of the organization, not among the people who run it. The machinery was the centerpiece. The employees were just the outer layer.

NASA continued to send people into space throughout the decades that followed, but it wasn't without additional casualties. There was the mid-air explosion of the space shuttle Challenger in 1986. Then in 2003, the crew of the Columbia died when the craft broke apart while re-entering earth's atmosphere. Once again, a review board was assembled to investigate. But this time the language used to explain the cause was notably different. While the report detailed the engineering-related failures, the board added a whole section about the culture of NASA as a contributing factor. Compare this to the language used just three decades earlier:

> "The organizational causes of this accident are rooted in the space shuttle program's history and culture, including the original compromises that were required to gain approval for the shuttle, subsequent years of resource constraints, fluctuating priorities, schedule pressures, mischaracterization of the shuttle as operational rather than developmental, and lack of an agreed national vision for human space flight. Cultural traits and organizational practices detrimental to safety were allowed to develop...."

In all, the Columbia report contained 137 uses of the word "culture," whereas the Apollo 1 and Challenger reports contained none. Zero. This attention to culture highlights a monumental shift in thinking, not just at NASA, but across the global workforce. The machinery was no longer the hero it once was. Instead, the machinery was taking its place within a larger construct, one that better explains what an organization is and how it functions.

I'd like to suggest that *culture* is now the concept that best defines how the various components in an organization come together and relate to each other. It's not just a reference to people, but it's also everything those people produce as organizational artifacts. And it includes the machinery itself which, after all, was also created by people. The term *culture* is the holistic encapsulation of the organizational entity. It's the summation of all its characteristics. Culture means *everything*! And while there may be a serendipitous double-entendre in that statement, the part I'm trying to emphasize is that culture *refers to* all the pieces that make up a given ecosystem. Everything an organization *does* is a by-product of what it *is* — the culture that exists across it. The whole cannot be separated from its parts.

Therefore, if you have a performance problem, it's best to think of it as a culture problem that affects performance. They're inseparable.

As long as people are the inventors, cultivators, managers, and perpetrators of business activities, the causation of those activities must be attributed to the culture that surrounds them.

The Financial Cost

So if culture isn't just lipstick and rouge for an organization… if it's central to the very identity of the organization… if it truly impacts performance and profit… then it's imperative to know what it costs in terms of tangible dollars. Damn the mysteries and ambiguities of psychology, this is costing us real money! We've got to find a way to measure it accordingly. I've observed that when board members begin to evaluate the financial implications of culture in today's workforce, the enigma of human behavior I mentioned earlier suddenly moves to the center of the strategic plan.

But how do you begin to quantify something as intangible as human engagement… or the dollar-cost of operating with a disengaged culture day after day?

Indulge me in a bit of mathematics. Gallup estimates that worker engagement in the U.S. is roughly 31%, and therefore 69% of the workforce is disengaged to one degree or another. Gallup also estimates that the cost to the American GDP of that 69% non-engagement is $500 billion.

Stay with me.

So if the American GDP is $18.5 trillion, it could be $19 trillion if 100% of workers were engaged — a difference of about 5%. In other words, the average company experiences about 5% reduction in total performance due to less-than-great worker engagement. (It's likely closer to the 31% I mentioned earlier. But we'll use the most conservative figures for now.) For a $1 billion company, that's a loss of $50 million every year. And that's an extremely conservative estimate.

In contrast, companies with great cultures have three times better employee engagement than those with undesirable cultures, a value of $33 million, using the above algorithm. In my experience, the culture of most $1 billion companies can usually be optimized by investing less than a tenth of that amount. In fact, using the model revealed later in this book, one of our clients (also a billion-dollar organization) saw a five-thousand-to-one payback from the amount they invested to optimize their culture.

So how do these numbers play out at your company? A watershed moment for many leaders is when they're able to calculate the dollar-value of engagement in their own organization. Here's the first formula you need to understand when it comes to culture:

$C = MVV \times L / Eng$

Culture equals your Mission, Vision and Values... multiplied across your Labor Force... then divided by the level of engagement of your people.

That's the formula for culture. Whether you've known this formula or not, it's been actively shaping the culture where you work all along. If you're a leader, your culture starts with the mission you've established, the vision you've cast, and the values you personify as a company. Most leaders know they need to write out these cornerstone ideals. But even if you've never actually done the exercise of determining your MVV, you've already got a culture that perfectly reflects them. Your mission may be as lofty as changing the world, or as plain as making money. However, whether it's expressed or implied, employees can usually tell what the company's all about. And if they're forced to figure it out themselves, they'll fill in the blanks the best they can. It'll either be something that inspires them or something they tolerate until they can land a better gig somewhere else.

Next in our equation, your culture is the byproduct of scaling that MVV across the entire labor force of the company. As the formula implies, MVV are modified by this step of the equation. The mission personified at the frontline by an hourly employee is quite different from the one written by the founder of the company. Make no mistake. By the time the words on that marble plaque reach the muddy trenches where the brand battles for market share, the language gets tweaked. The actual values your customers experience when interacting with your brand are a loose interpretation at best and a gross distortion at worst.

This brings us to the *Eng* part of the equation. The common denominator of every culture is Eng, or Engagement. This is the single greatest determiner of success or failure in the whole equation. Get this part right and the other pieces almost fall right into place. This is where the real work on culture happens. Solve engagement and you'll have the ability to put it to work on any number of missions or visions.

> *Despite what many leaders have been taught, mission, vision, and values are not the key to a strong culture.*

Are those things important? Absolutely. But if we're honest, thousands of leaders have done the hard work of writing eloquent statements that nobody remembers, much less connects to the work they do every day. That's because the approach is backwards. To lead effectively in today's world, you should first ask how the workforce is wired to be inspired. Companies do this instinctively with other resources. Nobody grows weeds and tries to pass them off as vegetables. Yet somehow when it comes to human resources, there's this notion that if you plant something and water it once in a while it should thrive.

I often wonder how the term *human resources* came to exist in the first place. It's almost an oxymoron. Is it really wise to think of people as mere resources? Granted, that approach is workable as long as the humans in question are desperate for survival and don't have the luxury of deciding how they're treated. But the world has changed a lot over the last several generations. Work used to represent a mere functional necessity. People didn't have a choice. So the companies who offered work could get by simply treating humans like inanimate resources. The American Dream changed all that. Over time, workers have come to expect more than just a paycheck. A lot more. They require dignity and respect… a future… and an identity as a meaningful contributor to something larger than even themselves. You see, humans have something other resources don't: *a soul.*

Organizations, being made up of people, take on a type of *collective soul.*

The Soul of the Organization

Precisely how do things like culture and human behavior affect performance for an organization? What is a collective soul? And what role does it really play in everyday operations?

These actually might be the most important questions in business today. You see, most leaders have exhausted all the other questions… the practical, tactical questions. Questions like, "Who's our customer?" "What's the strategy?" "Where's the market headed?" They've built complex algorithms to manage inventory levels. They've developed predictive analytics and created models for consumer behavior. They've amassed data to determine head count and span-of-control. Year after year, they gather all the experts in the room and put the PowerPoint slides on the screen. They review and explore and pontificate.

And yet, the question of human performance remains unanswered. Everything else is lifeless theory until the people — the geniuses and the weirdos and the in-between of the modern workforce — touch it and put it into action.

Perhaps you've been there. You've studied the vast nebulae that make up this universe called organizational effectiveness. You see the complex galaxies we call *management*. You recognize the clusters that comprise *leadership*. And no matter how long you look through that telescope, you can't seem to chart the infinite, unknown blackness that is human performance.

The people factor is unknown. A void.

No doubt Peter Drucker, the undisputed father of modern management, faced a similar void before writing *The End of Economic Man,* and *The New Society,* and *The Practice of Management.* Drucker was a mapmaker. A cartographer of the modern organization. He sailed the depths of organizational effectiveness where fabled monsters roamed and he brought back the first tools for navigation. Drucker wrote about management in high-definition. He followed intuition like a superhighway, and replaced conceptual vapor with a definitive lexicon. In the wake of his mastery, it's easy to forget that he once faced a void too. There were many times when he stared into the unknown. Thirty-nine times Drucker headed off into the wilderness and came back with a book to show us the way.

Truth be told, Drucker didn't finish the whole map. He couldn't. The organizational universe keeps expanding, adding variables, complexities, and exceptions. The tectonic plates of business are always shifting. The void keeps expanding. Changing. And now we, like Drucker, must consider which uncharted blackness requires mapping in order to achieve organizational effectiveness in our time. We stand on the time-tested principles of management. We frequent the familiar paradigms of leadership. And yet, we too have intersected with the unfinished highways that point toward the mysterious unknown. Our systems break. Our people fail to perform. Our customers don't respond. And we're left to wonder why. Could our maps of the organizational universe be incomplete? Is there a world beyond management and leadership?

If you think about it, management and leadership do little more than form a skeleton for an organization. It still must be inhabited by a more personified being. A brand and a personality. A culture. A soul.

When our first daughter was born, the umbilical cord was wrapped around her neck. Calmly, the doctor fixed the problem and reassured us that a surprising 10-30% of babies experience this issue. Nevertheless, it took a team of nurses several minutes to get our daughter going properly. I'll never forget her little body lying there. Perfectly formed. But lifeless. Billions of cells had managed to arrange themselves according to plan. An intricate system of delicate organs was ready to become human. But there was no child. The blue blob on the table seemed more like a science experiment than a person. Then, suddenly, a jolt surged through her body. A loud cry turned her skin bright pink. Her little face crinkled up in protest. She had personality. Attitude. A soul.

Companies come to life in a similar way. They're made up of buildings and machinery and systems. They're designed with intricate org charts made up of divisions and teams. They have management systems and leadership structures with skills for each discipline. But the vast majority of what they become is yet to be determined. It's the actual people who inhabit the company that determine its personality and attitude. Its soul.

Organizations, made up of people, tend to reflect the same human values and idiosyncrasies exhibited by those people. Collectively, they form the soul of the organization. This is important to acknowledge because that's where customers feel it: in their soul. They absorb all the experiences designed by the organization's strategies and procedures and they form what we like to call a *brand perception*. But if we were totally honest, we'd just call it a hunch. Because that's how most customers process it when they make purchase decisions. They have a hunch. Of course, the idea of a hunch doesn't play too well in most business settings. So brand perception it is. But let's not dismiss the reality that all business is ultimately a human proposition. It's decided upon by people. It's executed by people. That means it's subject to the influences of things like personality and attitude… soul.

> And culture is essentially the collective soul of the organization.

That collective soul — the culture — is more than just a sentimental apparition summoned to warm the cold, impersonal machinery of business. Culture is a corporate census of the psychology that runs the machinery. Culture indicates the state of mind from which the company's actions originate. It is impossible, therefore, to lead the culture of an organization without first quantifying that state of mind using some type of framework.

Drucker didn't talk a lot about culture. Nor should he have at that time. He was engrossed in documenting the landscape of a new industrialized world. Work itself was fundamentally different. Someone had to describe what was going on and create systems for functioning as an organization. It needed an operating system. That work fell to Drucker. He once reflected, "I had been working for 10 years consulting and teaching, and there simply was nothing or very little (about management). So I kind of sat down and wrote it, very conscious of the fact that I was laying the foundations of a discipline."

I'm writing this book because I've been working for more than 10 years consulting and teaching on culture, and there's very little that lays out the foundations of this important discipline. Yes, there are plenty of books that do a wonderful job of introducing the reader to superstar role models and inspiring principles. But if an average leader is to enter the workforce properly prepared to build culture, there needs to be a framework similar to those used to teach management or leadership. We need a thesis that promotes a worldview, and a set of rules for operating within it. Today's workforce is fundamentally different from anything we've seen before. We need a new operating system. This book lays out mine.

Culture: The New Frontier

I don't have to convince most leaders that culture is the number one issue on the business landscape today. For decades, it was management and leadership. They've tweaked and updated and reorganized over and over in hopes of smoothing out the rough spots and squeezing incremental performance out of their systems. But leadership principles can only be reinvented so much. Over the years, the returns on those efforts have been steadily diminishing. And little by little, organizations are turning to culture as the new frontier for improving performance. As I'll demonstrate later, they're absolutely right to do so.

But here's the problem. Culture has never really been quantified like the other organizational disciplines we leverage to run our companies. It's slippery and elusive. If you thought leadership was difficult to master, try getting your head around a topic that most people can't even define convincingly.

As a result, the people in charge of our organizations default to something they can fathom a little better — namely leadership. After all, it's been around long enough that even the average professional can talk the talk. Leadership knowledge has even made its way into the mainstream. You know it's ubiquitous when the public elementary school in my neighborhood is based entirely on Franklin Covey's *The Leader in Me*, a complete system for running a school. The elementary school where I grew up was based on how you shouldn't stick gum under your desk. Leadership is everywhere now. You can't walk past a Marriott ballroom these days without bumping into a motivational speaker preparing to give a keynote on it.

That's not the case with culture. The typical executive would struggle even to name all the factors that influence culture in his organization.

Sure, leaders know a lot about the *topic* of culture and how it gets reflected in the behaviors, rituals, and personality of a company. But there's not a disciplined *framework* that the average person can use to build a culture from the ground up.

A Holistic Proposition

Maybe you would include yourself among the leaders I'm talking about. You've read books and blogs and watched videos that share powerful insights and tips for fostering a healthy culture. You've taken the famous culture workshop at Zappos. You understand a number of the keys to improving the people factor across an organization. You've even applied several ideas successfully with noticeable results. More importantly, you've got significant natural instincts when it comes to troubleshooting engagement and resolving culture issues.

But most of what's available to leaders today enables them to influence culture only in isolated, and often temporary, ways. Not to mention, virtually all of this content takes an extrinsic behavioral approach, completely ignoring the complex, internal psychology that shapes values and drives innate behaviors. None of them endeavor to encompass all the factors that influence workplace culture or organize them into a single equation or a clear algorithm. As a result, leaders can get the basic idea of culture, but they aren't introduced to the levers that drive, adjust, or strengthen culture inside an organization.

With something as critical — and expensive — as Human Resources, you owe it to yourself to get this right. For most companies, labor cost is 20% to 35% of gross sales, on average. In the service sector, it's more like 50%. For one of my clients, it's even higher — over 70%. When it comes to culture and performance, the fate of the company is at stake. And yet, the vast majority of what passes for culture work today is like the pig's lipstick. The lipstick is often fantastic. But when the ham itself goes bad, everyone still gets food poisoning.

Learning to Fly

It's tempting to approach culture the way humans once approached the dream of flight. To see a bird gliding overhead makes flying seem so within reach. All you need are some wings and a source of propulsion. Right?

That's what the Wright brothers thought too. And it worked for almost five years. Everybody knows about the first flight at Kitty Hawk in 1903. It's the story we love to re-live: mankind reaches new heights of freedom and accomplishment. All it took was a set of wings and a propeller.

But on September 17, 1908, reality set in. Orville Wright and passenger Thomas Selfridge were circling the parade grounds above Fort Myer, Virginia. Nearly three thousand onlookers gathered below, none more enthusiastic than the lucky Selfridge, who at age 26 had recently dedicated himself to the new field of aviation as a Lieutenant in the signal corps. Wright agreed to take him up after numerous requests from the young officer. The flight began as expected, completing four laps around the field. Suddenly, the plane began lurching uncontrollably then dove nose-first into the ground. Selfridge died – the world's first aviation fatality.

Wright and Selfridge took off with a simplified understanding of aviation. As they spiraled toward earth, however, they brought with them a new respect for the myriad factors that needed to be mastered.

Today, pilots and passengers alike respect aviation as the complex undertaking it is. There's more to it than just a set of wings and a dream. A lot more.

The field of culture has followed a similar path. Early attempts to get morale off the ground were simplistic; a few helium-filled balloons to lift people's spirits, and a motivational speech to propel the team. In recent years, however, we've discovered there's more to it.

The field of aviation can teach us a lot about how to approach culture. In aviation, like culture, you can't afford to wing it. Think about the training required to operate a commercial jet. Millions of dollars and priceless human lives are hanging in the balance. The pilot must master a myriad of switches and dials and levers. More importantly, he must understand how they all work together to affect the craft in flight. He spends hours in simulations practicing a wide range of possible scenarios and perfecting the subtleties that affect a craft in flight.

Aviation is a holistic proposition. If you leave out even one of the critical elements, you could end up like Selfridge. That's why you can't receive a pilot's license just because you're really good at one or two aspects of flying a plane. You may know how to read the altimeter, or work the pitch wheel, or set the flaps. But in aviation, that's not good enough. Not even close. Because if you aren't skilled at everything, you could end up spiraling toward earth.

In contrast, many companies accept a piecemeal approach when it comes to culture. They check it off as satisfactory because they've drafted a set of core values, or spent millions on the office environment, or implemented a recognition program, or installed a performance management system. Each of those things can be great. But if you leave out even one of the critical elements, it can all come crashing down.

So let me ask you: Can you name all the factors that influence culture in your organization? Do you have a system that enables you to check the status of each one, the way a pilot goes over a checklist prior to take-off? When something goes wrong, can you pinpoint the cause? And provide an efficient remedy? Is your organization practiced at the important skills required to create a safe, successful, and inspiring experience for your people? Or do you kind of wing it?

This book is for everyone who's followed all the right thought-leaders, watched the right videos on TED.com, subscribed to the right blogs, and even been to workshops to learn the so-called secrets of culture, but you still don't know exactly how to lead the culture of your organization with confidence and certainty. You know several important keys, and you understand some of the core concepts quite well, but when it comes to drafting a comprehensive strategy for culture, you can't be certain there won't be gaps and unknown variables.

The premise behind this book is the simple idea that authentic culture — not the aspirational veneer some companies try to shoehorn onto their brand, but the honest, deeply-held sentiment of your people — is the result of subconscious impulses they encounter throughout the employee experience. These impulses determine the level of attention, effort, and sacrifice a person will exert in any given situation. They also determine their adherence to the values of the organization around them, whether those values are formally stated or merely implied through everyday behaviors. Best of all, they can be quantified! As a leader, you can monitor each of these factors the way a pilot scans the cockpit dials, giving you the confidence that you're creating a culture that perfectly complements your organizational strategies. For each of the factors that drive culture, there are corresponding practices that you can implement to impact the status of the factor… giving you the ability to build a strong culture, step by step.

The brain of every member of the workforce is constantly scanning for anything that impacts a person's well-being — things that either threaten or ensure survival, or that might present an opportunity to enhance their quality of life. The subconscious plays an intricate role in these computations. When a situation benefits us, we are drawn toward it. When it no longer benefits us, or even harms us, we withdraw and seek something else. Every employee in every organization is continually evaluating the workplace this way. Essentially, they're looking for two things: to ensure survival, and to leverage opportunity. This is the key to understanding both engagement and culture.

In order to build culture consistently and confidently, you must be able to manage all the factors that influence these impulses, not just the extrinsic behaviors. The system in this book is designed to help you do just that. Moreover, after implementing these concepts in companies across the country for more than a decade, I'm convinced they can enable any leader to foster engagement and culture, predictably and consistently. I've had opportunities to apply them in foodservice, healthcare, manufacturing, financial services, and real estate, to name a few verticals. Their impact is invaluable in virtually any situation where brand performance is dependent on the ability of large groups of people to function together, to generate consistent initiative, and to execute the mission of their organization.

A Hierarchy for Culture

As it turns out, the people inside an organization are just like the ones on the outside. They're customers too. And while they may not be in the market for the products and services you deliver, they are in the market for a host of other things that correspond to their needs. Things that you, their employer, can provide in exchange for valuable work.

This concept is fundamental to all business. Employees work in order to receive. But don't think for an instant that a paycheck satisfies their needs.

In fact, workers in a company have all kinds of needs. Survival needs, social needs, and transcendent needs. They won't stop until they're met, either. They may slow down from time to time — to punch the clock, to meet a few sales quotas, or shuffle some papers — but they won't stop. Their needs pull them like gravity toward the cravings they feel inside. And when the workplace doesn't offer what they're looking for, their souls begin to wander.

This is what some have called disengagement. It's when a company pays for a whole employee but only gets the hands and a little bit of the head, but not the heart. This is why engagement is the key to culture.

Culture is driven by engagement. Engagement is driven by the needs of the employees. And all needs can be organized into a system, or hierarchy. Abraham Maslow showed us how. And in the pages that follow I want to show you how that same hierarchy can be used to meet needs, engage your internal customers, and drive culture.

As Warren Buffett once cautioned, "The worst mistakes involve not understanding other people as well as you might."

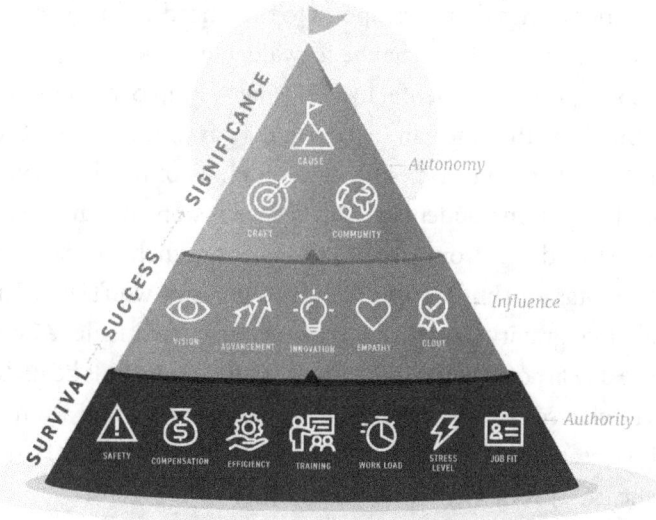

Reflect:
How well do you understand the concept of culture?

CHAPTER 2

IGNITING CULTURE

"A lot of the changes are so gradual that they don't even qualify as news, or even as interesting: they're so mundane that we just take them for granted. But history shows that it's the mundane changes that are more important than the dramatic 'newsworthy' events."

~ Robert D. Kaplan

Maybe Dan Cathy likes to play with fire. There was that time in 2002 when he soaked an enormous pile of brush cuttings with gasoline and lit a match. The vapor exploded, enveloping him in flames and earning him a helicopter ride to the burn unit at Grady Memorial Hospital in Atlanta. No, he wasn't a child. He was 48, and already the President of Chick-fil-A, a multi-billion-dollar restaurant brand. As he explains, "I love stepping out of the corporate world, even for a little bit, and getting my hands dirty."

The fire burned itself out and Cathy made a full recovery. But a decade later he would start a fire that wasn't as easy to contain.

The year was 2012, precisely a decade after the brush fire incident. There would be no matches or gasoline involved this time. No brush either. This was the kind of fire that doesn't need accelerants to rage out of control. As the biblical writer James put it thousands of years ago, "The tongue is a fire." Cathy's tongue would prove to be a flamethrower.

He was a guest on the Ken Coleman Show, a syndicated talk radio program I co-hosted briefly. By now, Cathy had become an icon of corporate leadership, and he was invited to discuss the principles he uses in business. For good reason too. He wasn't just the heir of Truett Cathy, the restaurant's legendary founder. In fact, despite the enormous shadow cast by his father, Dan had quietly carved a reputation of his own by leading the company from a regional novelty into one of the top players in the industry. And it wasn't dumb luck. With expert proficiency, he took the brand's southern charm and codified it into a system that has become the envy of organizations everywhere. Whenever Chick-fil-A opens a new restaurant, a magical community of bright, attentive employees seem to materialize out of thin air. Aspiring customers camp out for days to take part in the Grand Opening. The growth isn't just from market expansion either. Existing Chick-fil-A units seem to explode in growth year after year. No matter how busy they get (picture double drive-thru lanes wrapped around the building while, simultaneously, the dining room hosts a capacity crowd as patrons enter and exit the building on queue) they somehow remain staffed at just the right levels to match the onslaught of business.

How do you do that? How does anyone do that in a world as fragmented and distracted and competitive as the workplace today? If you'd asked Dan Cathy how they do it at Chick-fil-A, ten seconds wouldn't elapse between the end of your question and the first utterance of the word *leadership*.

The Leadership Business

If you're someone in charge of other people, or building customer loyalty, or leading effective teams, or attracting and retaining talent… you already know what I'm talking about. The name Chick-fil-A is synonymous with leadership. For many business people, it's a flag on a hill… a standard to shoot for… an example to study. Despite its sometimes incendiary politics and inflammatory religious views, the brand has accomplished things anyone in business can appreciate. And the skills of leadership sit at the very center of it all. You can see it in the way their employees carry themselves. It's measurable in the speed of their drive-thru lines. And it's indisputable in their record-breaking sales.

I had the fortune of being on the inside at Chick-fil-A during some of their most important leadership initiatives. Most significantly, I was hired to write and produce several courses of training on leadership and culture. I was privy to the road maps that saw Chick-fil-A rocket from a folksy regional chain to the third-largest restaurant company in the US. On my first visit to headquarters, stores were selling an average of $2.5 million annually. As of this writing, the average is closer to $10 million per store.

Same store footprint, almost triple the throughput.

Much of Chick-fil-A's rapid growth is attributed to their knack for talent, which drives the trademark customer experience and enthusiastic fan base. Almost everywhere I go, leaders want to know Chick-fil-A's secret. How did they establish such impressive brand consistency? Where do they find all those winsome teenage employees? What's the key to keeping everyone aligned throughout such astounding growth and unprecedented change?

A big part of the answer is their commitment to developing leaders. For decades Chick-fil-A has been investing heavily to build leadership principles into the fiber of the brand. They've partnered with leadership gurus like Jim Collins, John Maxwell, John Wooden, Seth Godin, Patrick Lencioni, Henry Cloud, Andy Stanley, and Ken Blanchard. They've licensed leadership content from the library curated by *Harvard Business Review*. They've crafted their own company leadership model, an adaptation of Kouzes and Posner's classic *Leadership Challenge*. For many years they sponsored a glitzy annual conference called LeaderCast, which grew to over 50,000 attendees worldwide. Chick-fil-A doesn't really see themselves as being in the restaurant business. To quote one of their most senior executives, "We're in the leadership business… we just happen to sell chicken sandwiches."

As I watched the brand skyrocket to success, it seemed clear that leadership was a wonder drug for organizational health. It was the magic elixir that cured any common ailment.

But I want to share a Dan Cathy story you probably haven't heard before. This story shatters the theory that leadership is a cure-all. Because of it, I came to realize that leadership is actually just the syringe, not the actual medicine.

Back to the 2012 "fire" I mentioned:

Playing Chicken

The radio interview between Ken Coleman and Dan Cathy began as a light discussion of current events and the principles of business. Without much thought, Dan began telling the host about the values that drive him professionally. In the process, he drifted down a rabbit trail and began sharing his personal beliefs about same-sex marriage, a topic that was dominating headlines at the time. Dan summarized what he called, "the biblical definition of the family unit," and went on to suggest that alternative lifestyles were the result of, "a prideful, arrogant attitude."

It may seem strange that a leadership interview ended up on the topic of same-sex marriage. But it did. And in the process, it exposed the profound vulnerability of leadership itself: that it wields in equal measure the power to create or to destroy.

Within days, Cathy's statements about gay marriage began to surface in the news. Excerpts of the interview were repeated by CNN, the *Los Angeles Times*, the *Washington Post*, and the Associated Press. On social media, numerous groups lashed out at Cathy over his intolerance of alternative lifestyles. Instantly, Chick-fil-A found itself at the center of a national controversy.

In an attempt to head off the growing story, Cathy accepted an interview with the Baptist Press, a news organization generally viewed as an ally to the company. In all sincerity, Dan is one of the wisest leaders I've ever seen in action. His father, Truett, was a man way ahead of his time. Their legacy gave one the impression that good instincts just run in the Cathy family. So when Dan finally stepped up to answer his accusers, I thought the matter would be quickly resolved. Surely he would make overtures of humility and compassion sufficient to satisfy the growing din of protests.

He did no such thing.

Rather than disarm the situation with tactful statements, Cathy's words fanned the flames. Most of it happened when the reporter asked Dan if Chick-fil-A supports "the traditional family." Glibly, Cathy responded, "Guilty as charged." Maybe what Dan *meant* his comments to convey was something like, "I'm in support of all people experiencing the benefits that can come from a healthy, loving family." But what people heard *instead* might as well have been, "Like I said, if you're not from a traditional family, you don't line up with God's definition." Based on the way people interpreted his statements, you would have thought he was saying they could all just go to hell. So much for tact.

This was the early days of "cancel culture." Leaders like Dan had no idea just how much the world was changing.

This time the media attacked. Dan Cathy sound bites blared on every major news network. Advocates of same-sex marriage were irate, and they were out to silence the company once and for all. Protests were organized in front of restaurants around the country. A number of celebrities and other prominent people called for an all-out boycott of Chick-fil-A unless Cathy recanted his archaic views.

At headquarters, normal routines essentially stopped as the organization scrambled to understand the implications of what was happening. Many on the inside wondered if the company could withstand the growing storm. There were closed-door meetings all over the building. A paralyzing hush seemed to fall across the campus.

For Don Perry, the Director of Public Relations, it was a worst-case scenario. Don was an easy-going fellow who had worked at Chick-fil-A for nearly thirty years. He had often been the friendly spokesperson for the brand, issuing publicity statements or announcing new initiatives. But the weight of the media millstone grew heavier each day. Suddenly, tragically, Don suffered a fatal heart attack. One couldn't help wondering if it was related to the stress of trying to keep things from unraveling. The whole situation seemed hopeless.

As if those developments weren't shocking enough, what happened next was downright surreal.

When Culture Surpassed Leadership

It began as a sympathetic wave. A handful of loyal customers started reaching out to the company with gestures of encouragement. Cards and letters poured into headquarters. Sure, these people liked the food at Chick-fil-A. But it was much deeper than that. Somehow, they felt an emotional connection to the company. They respected the uncompromising commitment to values like "Closed on Sunday." They recognized the mastery with which employees executed each task. Perhaps it restored their faith in the American work ethic to see a job well done. Whatever their motivation, the flood of support soon resulted in a wave of calls, cards, and letters— some even rumored to contain money— sent in by everyday fans of the brand who wanted to help the company survive the ordeal. Methodically, Chick-fil-A returned each check to its sender with a note of thanks.

The outpouring reached a frenzied peak when then-governor of Arkansas, Mike Huckabee, declared an official "Chick-fil-A Day" to be observed nationwide in support of the restaurant and its traditional values. When the day came, the turnout was enormous. Cars lined up for blocks at many stores as guests awaited their turn to purchase a meal. All over the country, the scene was the same. Millions of Americans made purchases to show their support. In that one day, sales for the company were higher than any other day in the brand's history.

That's right, instead of losing business, Chick-fil-A set a new record!

The world is full of stories of rogue leaders taking down an entire company. It's so familiar that it hardly surprises us when it happens. After all, leaders *lead*. That's what they do. As the leader goes, so goes the company. But that's not what was happening with Chick-fil-A at all. In fact, it was the opposite! Somehow, thousands of everyday constituents — from politicians and customers to hourly workers — were essentially taking over. They not only made up for Dan Cathy's leadership miscue, they pushed the company into record territory.

One of the responsibilities of a leader is to protect his people from unnecessary duress. And while Dan Cathy was only trying to reinforce the values that drive his company, he should have done that without exposing his people to the attacks that he unwittingly provoked. In the leadership column on the stat sheet, Chick-fil-A lost yardage on that play. For most organizations, the damage it caused would have cost hundreds of millions, if not put them out of business completely.

But Chick-fil-A had a secret weapon.

So what was this strange force of nature that rescued Chick-fil-A from leadership disaster? Where did it come from, and how did it manage to out-influence the actions of the leader? What science might be used to fathom its movements?

As I'm sure you've surmised by now, it was the culture of Chick-fil-A that turned this leadership gap into the greatest milestone in the brand's history. I'll finish unpacking the building blocks of culture later — what they are and how they work — but I want to focus on something else first. Because there's a critical observation I hope you take away from this story. If you look carefully, it points to a profound shift in the dynamics that govern organizations everywhere. And as I'll argue in the pages that follow, this shift is the culmination of an evolution that goes all the way back to the Industrial Revolution. It marks a changing of the guard in our understanding of how employees are managed, how companies are run, and how business is conducted.

Peter Drucker, the father of modern management, predicted moments like this in some of his earliest writings: "Culture eats strategy for breakfast," he wrote. He could have added, "Culture eats leadership for lunch." In the complex molecular process that produces employee performance, culture — not leadership — is the primary element.

Culture has more power to influence outcomes than the leaders at the top or the strategies they devise.

Granted, leaders play a critical role in shaping culture, but once it gets going, the chain reaction of culture can change the landscape more dramatically than the actions of a leader.

As much as Chick-fil-A's *leadership* impacted things in 2012, it was Chick-fil-A's *culture* that ultimately determined the outcome.

> "Culture has surpassed leadership in its ability to determine organizational outcomes."

This brings me to the main point I'm trying to make: culture has surpassed leadership in its ability to determine organizational outcomes. And while that may seem obvious at first, don't run past the fact that it hasn't always been this way. When you examine the history of the workplace, a clear progression is evident. For decades — from the 1950s and 60s right up until a few years ago — leadership has been the key determiner of organizational success. But that's not the case anymore. And it changes everything about how to approach work itself. For you personally, in your career. And for the company where you work.

Whatever leadership represented to business in the past, it is slowly being replaced. Culture is the new leadership.

The Three Stages of a Company

Most leaders want to do great work and make a positive impact in people's lives. Unfortunately, the more success and growth they experience, the more strain it puts on the culture they work so hard to create. Employees become disengaged, retention plummets, and before they know it, performance is flat as the organization seems to collapse under the weight of its own success.

I referred to these legs earlier. But here's how it happens in a growing company.

Every company starts out in the Product Phase. Success in this phase is a simple reflection of the strength of the concept behind your products or services. When there's demand for your idea, the company grows. Congratulations, you've cleared the first hurdle. As momentum continues to rise, it's not long until someone has the notion to scale the idea. That leads us to phase two.

The second phase is the Process Phase. Success in this phase is a reflection of how well you create systems and processes that turn your idea into an operational business. If you produce more, and do it efficiently, the company grows yet again.

Then something strange happens. After months or years of cyclical growth, things start to level off. Every program produces diminishing returns. There are meetings attempting to identify the glass ceiling and get things back on track. The COO thinks operations are the key. After all, systems are what grew the company from a startup to an industry contender. Others kick the tires in the marketplace, fiddle with marketing, or analyze the competition in search of additional market share. It's hard to diagnose because anywhere you look there are gaps to close. And rather than finding one or two keys to driving growth again, it's more like a large, wet blanket hangs over the entire company, weighing everything down. That's what it feels like to slowly become an "organization." And that brings us to the third phase.

The third phase is the People Phase. Success in this phase is determined by your ability to foster engagement, encourage collaboration, and build a sense of authentic dedication to the company's mission. Tweaking operations won't do it. Improving the product won't help. You have to master the skills that influence people's performance. In fact, once a company reaches this phase, the most important thing they accomplish is simply existing as a functional group of people; it far surpasses whatever mastery it takes to produce their products or deliver their services.

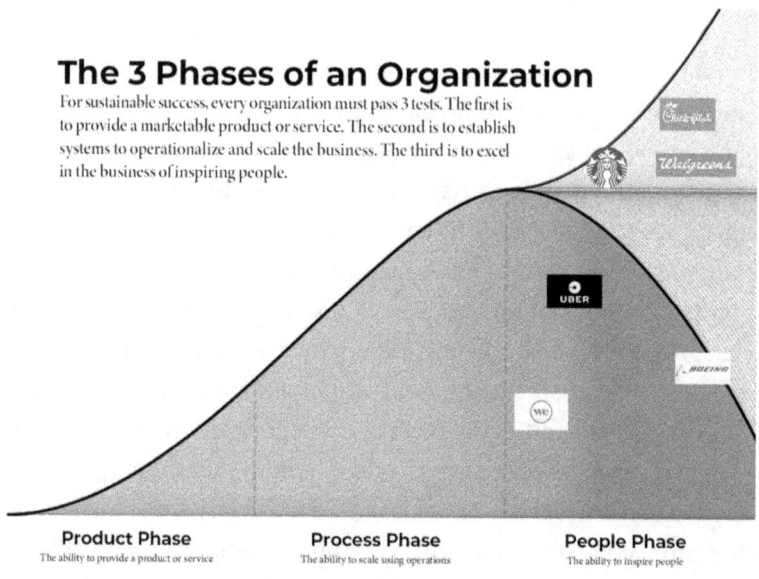

Every growing company experiences this three-stage metamorphosis. The culture starts out great, which helps to fuel growth. Growth transforms the culture and inevitably creates a drag that slowly becomes impossible to counteract. It's happened to some really good companies, including Starbucks, Eckerd, Best Buy, and Home Depot. Their success led to rapid growth, until they began to strain under the weight of the organization it created. Brand equity eroded, and market share declined. This is a tremendous frustration for leaders.

Fortunately, there's a solution. And some of the most respected brands have been using it to turn culture into their greatest asset. I want to show you how it can work for you too.

Reflect:
What brands stand out to you because of their culture?

CHAPTER 3

A BRIEF HISTORY OF WORK

"The world is changing very fast. Big will not beat small anymore. It will be the fast beating the slow."

~ Rupert Murdoch

To better understand where we are and what led us to this place, it's time to go all the way back to the beginning, to see where we've been, and how we got like this.

The corporate landscape today is unlike anything mankind has ever known. The tried-and-true approaches for running a company are proving less and less reliable. Traditional American organizations are finding themselves surrounded by a generation of people they don't understand. To make matters worse, the world has gotten bigger. Change happens faster. And one wrong tweet can bring a company to its knees. Since the 1950s, leadership has been the rudder that guides an organization to its destination. But as I demonstrated earlier, leadership skills alone are no longer enough.

There has to be an explanation.

Just a little over a hundred years ago, we were an agrarian society. Think about that for a moment. In 1900, the U.S. population was a little over 76 million. 30 million of those - nearly half - were farmers. Another large group was employed in roles that supported farming in one way or another. All told, the largest segment of our labor force was engaged in some form of agriculture-related activity. Just a couple of generations ago, people everywhere worked the land. That's astounding!

Think about the oldest person you ever met; it's probably someone born in the 1900s. If you're over fifty, there's a good chance you've met someone born in the late 1800s. Now think about the oldest person they ever met in their lifetime; it could have been someone born in the mid-1800s, before the Civil War! That's how recent we're talking. For that generation, there were no grocery stores like we have today, no refrigerators, indoor plumbing, air travel, cars, televisions, phones, drive-thru windows, or freeways between towns. Simply finding something to eat was a primary undertaking each day. And without modern storage and transportation systems, the majority of their food had to be procured locally. Most people rarely ventured more than two or three miles from home. Today, it's not uncommon to drive hundreds of miles into unknown territory without giving a second thought to things like food and water. But back then, you couldn't travel twenty miles without a plan for logistics. More on this thought later.

When the Renaissance and the Age of Enlightenment came along, people began placing a big emphasis on thinking. They were studying Greek philosophy, evaluating art, and experimenting with science. All throughout the 1700s and 1800s, the intellectual capital of the world was building up like magma inside a volcano. Finally, as the 19th century came to a close, the collective intelligence from all those years erupted in an explosion of inventions: steam engines, sewing machines, telephones, light bulbs, radios, cars, and airplanes. Everywhere you looked, new industries were being born. Steel was needed to make all kinds of products. Trains were needed to move the steel. Factories were needed to build the trains. Workers were needed to build the factories. Transportation was needed to bring the workers. Even food became an industry, with farm machines replacing the need for manual tilling, planting, and harvesting.

Almost overnight, workers walked out of the fields and into the factories. It was called the Industrial Revolution. With the invention of the assembly line, the labor force of an entire city was condensed into a single building.

First Came Management

Not since the pyramids were built had so many human resources been concentrated into such dense groups, and even then it wasn't on this scale. But to make it work, somebody had to organize and coordinate it. The work force needed an organizational discipline — an operating system — that could give it structure. And so the field of management was born.

For the first time in history, work itself became something to work on - a commodity to be managed and optimized. Never before had people been hired just to think about how everybody else works. This must have been a bizarre time for some as they reconciled the notion of paying thinkers higher salaries than the ones who actually did the work.

For the next several decades, some very smart people observed and wrote and tried to get their heads around what it all meant. Guys like Peter Drucker, Henri Fayol, and Max Weber developed intricate theories for leveraging the output of thousands of people at a time. Drucker, who wrote 39 books that helped define modern management, popularized the term "knowledge worker" to describe this new category of professional.

Understand that prior to the Industrial Revolution, there was no formal discipline called management. With the exception of government entities and a few European banks, the world was made up almost entirely of cottage businesses. There was no Fortune 500. There were no global chains. Managing ranks of people, as we know it, had existed only in military circles. There simply wasn't a big need to coordinate hundreds or even thousands of employees.

But the Industrial Revolution changed all that. And somebody had to invent an organizational operating system to make it all work. Management became that system. Once again, consider the statement I referenced earlier from Peter Drucker, "I wrote The Practice of Management because there was no book on management. I had been working for 10 years consulting and teaching, and there simply was nothing or very little. So I kind of sat down and wrote it, very conscious of the fact that I was laying the foundations of a (new) discipline."

For roughly fifty years, the new operating system of management produced remarkable returns for companies. The concepts it introduced fueled a new era in business. Where hard work had always been the ultimate measure of output, smart work became the new standard. Words like productivity and efficiency reshaped the workplace lexicon and became areas of focus for specialized executives. As their understanding of organizational principles grew, companies gained an extraordinary new capacity to coordinate massive operations and to mobilize vast numbers of people. The idea of scaling the business took on a whole new meaning. Thanks to the invention of corporate management, the number of large organizations rose dramatically during the 1900s. Global corporations number in the thousands today. But before this point in history, they were almost unimaginable.

Even the U.S. government began reflecting the management mindset, layering its principles on top of the foundations set by the Founding Fathers. To rescue America from the Great Depression, President Franklin D. Roosevelt leveraged this operating system when he enacted the "New Deal" to create jobs and stimulate productivity nationwide. Many of the principles of FDR's plan were drawn directly from the ideas embraced by successful corporations. They worked too. A nation is a type of organization, and it has components that function much like the others. It's made up of people whose interactions adhere to an operating system. In fact, wherever groups of people are interacting in a constructive manner, you'll find there's an operating system in place to coordinate their efforts. The New Deal was such a plan for the country. And it borrowed concepts from basic management theory.

By the 1950s and 60s, the experts had pretty much mastered the discipline of management. They'd leveraged Drucker's concepts for every possible advantage. Over time, management practices were familiar just about everywhere. New insights were published from time to time, but for the most part the landscape stabilized as the existence of knowledge workers became the new normal. And as happens with all innovations, the incremental returns on management began to diminish.

Of course companies were still looking for additional ways to get ahead of their competitors. If the other guys were also practicing management, what could they do to out-manage them? If management was the new normal, what was next?

Then Came Leadership

About that time, another significant development began. Thought-leaders like Warren Bennis began to notice that the competency of a senior executive - the person in charge of management itself - could have an enormous impact on the output of the company. Believe it or not, this was counterintuitive at the time. Up to this point, the focus had been on managing the productivity of workers and the efficiency of systems. The idea of leadership existed, but the notion of cultivating it didn't. The workplace was ripe for a new organizational discipline that would enable them to take things to the next level.

And so a new operating system — leadership — was born. Leadership was to management like Windows was to DOS. DOS is still there, but Windows runs on top of it. Similarly, management hasn't gone away. But leadership runs on top of it.

Smart people began observing, measuring and testing new hypotheses. They analyzed both the successes and the failures of the leaders in charge and reverse-engineered the critical steps. Before long, they identified a set of skills that formed this new field. And throughout the 1970s and 80s, the word "leadership" began to buzz inside the halls of academia. Eventually, their thoughts began to populate the bookstores. As leaders mastered those skills, the returns were significant. For half a century, they fueled the growth of industries and the careers of executives. Then, as had happened with management disciplines, the incremental returns of leadership disciplines began to taper off.

That's the 20th Century in a nutshell. Fifty years in the era of management followed by fifty years in the era of leadership. Which brings us to the next era and its challenges - an era we're still in today.

Then Came Woodstock

The way I see it, the kick-off of the next era — and the one we're still in today — was celebrated on a single weekend back in 1969. By some bizarre coincidence, I was actually there. Sort of. Let me explain.

Back then I was just a little kid in the jump seat of the family station wagon, facing backwards and peering out the rear window as we drove along. For summer vacation that year we drove from our home on Lookout Mountain, Tennessee to New York City for a family reunion in the house where my father grew up. The final part of our trip took us out of the city to see some old friends before heading home. As we rode along, my mother was dressed in a polyester travel suit. My big sisters read comic books in the middle row. Surrounded by luggage, I watched the Manhattan skyline shrink in the distance as we made our way into the lush, green countryside of upstate New York.

I spent a lot of time in the back of that car as a kid. I watched the world like a movie playing in reverse. When you spend your childhood staring back at where you've just been, you can't help thinking about why things turn out like they do. It's probably why I'm writing about all this in the first place.

As our station wagon crossed the Sullivan County line, we crested a hill and traffic suddenly stopped. My mother let out a prolonged gasp like she'd seen a UFO. My sisters were silent. When I turned around, the landscape I saw looked like a refugee camp. There were cars everywhere... along the edge of the woods, beside the roadway, or out in a nearby pasture. As far as you could see, people were just kind of walking around.

Our station wagon inched forward. I could hear loud guitar music blaring up ahead. I saw girls dancing on the hood of a car. A group of boys was using a tree for a urinal. Picnic blankets covered the grassy median where couples engaged in long, dramatic kisses. A girl puffed on a funny looking pipe, then blew the smoke right in her boyfriend's face. He inhaled deeply, like it was his favorite smell.

My mother told us to lock the doors.

For two hours, the traffic hardly moved. Four hours passed. Then six. Many people just got out, locked up their cars and walked away. Eventually the whole day passed and our trip was postponed. We were stranded at one of the biggest events of the 20th century: a rock festival known as Woodstock. Half a million people were jamming the New York Thruway to get to the concert. There we were, a traditional little family from the Bible belt, inadvertently deposited in the middle of the largest gathering of hippies at the height of the counterculture movement. I felt like Beaver Cleaver in an episode of That 70s Show.

Talk about culture shock.

My dad had a master's in sacred music and was known internationally as a classical composer and conductor. My mother was the daughter of a Methodist minister and an accomplished violinist. Needless to say, my parents didn't know much about rock and roll or the people who followed it. If they had, they definitely would have picked a different route to get to upstate New York. But they were clueless. So for one unforgettable weekend in 1969, we were part of music history, though not in any of the ways my conservative parents would have envisioned.

A change was taking place.

It would be decades later that I realized our little family had wandered into Ground Zero of the greatest shift of the workforce since the Industrial Revolution. That's right, music and politics weren't the only things shifting at Woodstock. The workforce was shifting too.

Here's what I mean.

Woodstock is considered the climactic expression of what the hippie movement was all about. Sure, there were many other iconic moments from the era: Haight-Ashbury, Altamonte, and Kent State, to name a few. But none captured the essence of what that generation of people was trying to communicate more accurately than Woodstock.

It was advertised as, "Three days of peace and music." But Woodstock stood for something much deeper than that simple tagline. It represented the personification of a movement whose broader theme was, "turn on, tune in, drop out," a phrase popularized by hippie leader Timothy Leary. The phrase conveyed the three guiding thoughts that emerged throughout the 60s and became a rally cry whose influence is still felt today. "Turn on" was a reference to the role hallucinogenic drugs played in rethinking the American way of life of the 50s and early 60s. A segment of the population had become repulsed by the effects of our industrialized world: commercialism, large-scale economics, and materialism. An acid trip was about as far away from those realities as a person could get. "Tune in" was a call to get back in touch with what the industrial machine was doing to people not only politically, but personally and socially, and perhaps even spiritually. "Drop out" meant to detach oneself from the establishment, so as not to condone or support the direction it was taking things.

In Woodstock, we see a generation of people having grown so disillusioned with the lifestyle awaiting them after college that they would rather just withdraw to a remote place in the countryside in hopes of finding peace.

They were disengaged!

It was more than just a protest against war and politics. It was a radical rejection of everything conventional society stood for. Even the polished wardrobe of the 50s was abandoned for long hair, tattered jeans, and tie-dye clothes. Also jettisoned was the American idea of working one's way up through a company to build a future. They wanted nothing to do with it. They preferred the idea of communes where people lived together and shared everything openly. And so in a way, Woodstock became the first documented outbreak of workplace disengagement on a massive scale.

More importantly, Woodstock was not just an artifact of a fringe population. All hippies were part of a generation known as the baby boomers. And while the rest of that generation might not have turned to drugs or anti-war protests, they shared much of the same inner sense of dissatisfaction, though they expressed it in more subtle ways.

Woodstock remains the largest single display of disengagement in American history. And it happened twenty years before anyone started measuring it.

The hippie movement seemed to die off soon enough, replaced by a decade of disco, then a decade of excess. But I'm convinced the sentiment of the hippie movement never really died. They just learned to suppress it a bit. Hippies and baby boomers alike made an unspoken treaty with society. In exchange for some moderate stability and gainful employment, they agreed to cut their hair, lay off the hard stuff, and commute to work each day. After all, they too wanted to live indoors, get married, and raise families.

So while most hippies eventually found their way into the workforce, their fundamental disenchantment with "the establishment" never completely faded. For the next two decades, their allegiance to the American economic system waffled. At times they seemed almost inspired to be part of a booming economy. But their commitment was tenuous, and their performance would often erode unless everything was just right. Almost anything could trigger a lull in their output - a sluggish economy, disagreements with management, or spring fever. Somehow they didn't quite possess that indefatigable, unshakeable work ethic that had characterized so many generations of workers before them. What was missing?

By no means am I suggesting that our current disengagement epidemic was caused by hippies entering the workforce and slowly infecting it with their "turn on, tune in, drop out" values. It's the other way around. I'm saying that there was something bigger beneath the surface of the population, and it was slowly shifting the mindset of every people group. The hippie movement - along with Woodstock - was just a more pronounced expression of the change that was brewing. It was the canary in the coal mine. The reality is that everyone's values were changing. And this change affected everything about the way they interacted with the economy and the workplace.

Tuned Out, Stepped On, Laid Off

As if the general malaise felt by baby boomers wasn't enough, things were about to get even worse. Because on top of everything else, the very makeup of the marketplace was shifting from a manufacturing economy to a service economy — a natural macroeconomic trend known as "structural transformation." It's driven by a combination of factors.

First is the simple idea that the richer a population gets, the greater their demand for services. Instead of doing everything themselves - mowing the grass, filing their taxes, or preparing dinner - they simply hire someone else to do it for them.

Second is something known as "the fracturing of vertical integration" that happens whenever an industry becomes commonplace. In a stable economy, specialists pop up in all kinds of places offering to perform certain business functions better and much cheaper than a company could do them internally. Over time in an established economy, industry processes can get refined many times over. Eventually companies are outsourcing more and more of their processes to service partners. The longer a manufacturing process exists, the more it tends to become fragmented, modularized, and eventually commoditized into interchangeable pieces. This is how Eli Whitney came to invent the cotton gin and offered the service of processing cotton to manufacturers in the textile industry. It's how Joseph Biedenharn began the service of providing glass bottles for soda manufacturer Coca-Cola. Manufacturers create systems, then outsiders insert themselves by improving segments of the process. For example, a car bearing a Ford emblem today might include parts from a metal stamping plant in the midwest, an alternator from a company in Texas, a radio made in Japan, and upholstery from a company in Central America. And each time the baton is passed between these entities, there's also a host of shipping, communications, bookkeeping, staffing, marketing, logistics and other services. That's a far cry from Henry Ford's vertically-integrated factories.

In its mature state, a manufacturing process might include a dozen or more service entities for every manufacturing one. The more an economy matures, the more sophisticated and complex it tends to become. And as it does, it gradually moves along the continuum from manufacturing basic goods, to providing value-enhancing services.

When the Industrial Revolution came along, it essentially pushed the reset button on the world economy. It reinvented the way things were manufactured. And in the process, it restarted the cycle of structural transformation for industries everywhere. In 1947, the service sector accounted for 60% of the jobs in the United States. Today that number is approaching 90%. Since 1977, the number of manufacturing jobs has dropped by more than 40%.

Unfortunately for baby boomers, structural transformation really began accelerating in the 80s and 90s, greatly disrupting what should have been the heyday of their career accomplishments. The core manufacturing jobs that had been the staple of the economy were being eliminated, and those who couldn't reinvent themselves were left behind. For those who had been reluctant to join the establishment in the first place, this would turn out to be the last straw.

As corporations adjusted to the changing landscape, they began moving the pieces of their processes around the chess board. Entire departments were outsourced, offshored, merged, or eliminated altogether. Jobs were downsized. And pension plans were revoked, leaving long-tenured employees without a plan for retirement. Baby boomers were caught up in the crossfire. If a portion of the workforce had already been jaded deep down inside, structural transformation served to yank the rug completely out from under them.

This perfect storm of factors gradually pushed the topic of employee engagement from one of general interest to primary concern. By the mid 1990s, it was emerging as the hottest issue in organizational effectiveness.

Living Off The Brand

So as you can see, the concept of employee engagement didn't begin with Gallup's Q12 study in 1990. Companies have been measuring employee happiness and well-being since the 1800s. It's had different names over the years — employee satisfaction, morale, commitment, happiness, sentiment, etc. But the basic concept is the same: How much are you into your job? Because if you're into it, you're more likely to perform better. Or as one adage puts it: an employee half-engaged is half an employee.

> *"People are either living for the brand or they're living off the brand."*

The best axiom for engagement I've ever heard came from Dan Cathy. He suggests that people are either living *for* the brand or they're living *off* the brand. That pretty much describes it for me. In vibrant cultures, there's a sense that the energy is flowing *from* the people *to* the brand. They live for it. In toxic cultures, it's the other way around. The energy flows *from* the brand *to* the people. They're living off it like just another form of welfare. Get too many of this kind and they'll suck the life out of the company.

By 1990 disengagement had become pandemic enough that Gallup then got the idea to begin measuring it. But the idea of living *off* the brand instead of *for* the brand had been there all along. Gallup simply helped to connect morale to performance, which put a dollar sign next to what it was costing companies. Gallup's Q12 study compared the performance of engaged and actively disengaged employees and showed that the ones who scored in the top half on employee engagement had twice the success of those in the bottom half. Moreover, the 99th percentile was four times more successful than the first percentile. The study also quantified the effect on turnover, safety, and quality.

The World Is Flat And So Is Engagement

There are all kinds of things you could say about the ongoing disengagement pandemic. For starters, as has already been discussed ad nauseam, fewer than one-third of the workforce qualifies as "engaged." Many people still seem to enjoy marveling over that fact. And truly, it is a reality that we should find not only shocking, but perhaps even shameful. For all our pontificating on management and leadership - Amazon currently lists more than 74,000 titles on the category - why are we getting such low grades from the people we're managing and leading? If this were a movie on Netflix, it would have an audience score of 31% from Rotten Tomatoes. That's worse than all five movies in the Twilight series! It's one thing to watch a movie like that, but it's another thing to go to work there every day.

But that's not the astounding part. There's something even more shocking that is almost never discussed. According to Gallup, the number of engaged/disengaged workers has stayed virtually THE SAME for over thirty years! Gallup acknowledged it this way back in 2015:

"Employee engagement entered a rather static state [again] in 2015 and has not experienced large year-over-year improvements in Gallup's 15-year history of measuring and tracking the metric. Employee engagement has consistently averaged less than 33%."

That's great news for the consulting industry. It means the stream of sick companies needing help shows no signs of drying up. But if you're a business owner, or if you own stock in a company, or if you have a job working at one of these places, it's horrifying.

Plenty has been published about what disengagement costs companies. But very little is mentioned about how much has been spent since 1990 on fixing disengagement - evidently all in vain. On the conservative end, let's just say it's 10% of the $450 billion global revenues for the consulting industry. That's not counting anything companies invest internally - HR efforts, incentive programs, performance management systems, etc. The latter easily matches the former. That's a total of $90 billion. Each year! By those estimates, we've spent roughly $1.5 trillion on engagement since Gallup first called our attention to the problem in 1990. And the statistics on engagement haven't budged. That's like putting your money in a vending machine and getting nothing out of it - thirty years in a row!

I can't help thinking we're missing something. How could such intelligent creatures come up short so consistently? This is the same species that figured out how to put a man on the moon in less than a decade and it only cost us $20 billion! But somehow we keep throwing money at disengagement oblivious to the fact that we aren't making progress.

Human psychology is a fascinating thing. It holds the answers to all kinds of astounding behaviors. It's the theater for some of the most remarkable phenomena in the world. In psychology lie the reasons one man volunteers to risk his life for his country while another takes his own life in a suicide bombing. Psychology explains why an athlete endures torturous conditions all for the hope of having a medal placed around his neck. In psychology are found all the passions and motives that drive people.

Perhaps psychology can explain how employees who once endured unthinkable conditions for the opportunity to work became a population that's working for the weekend.

Reflect:
How have you seen the workplace change?

CHAPTER 4

CULTURE HAPPENS

"Everybody has a plan until they get punched in the mouth."

~ Mike Tyson

The purpose of this book is to share the fundamental principles that will, once and for all, take culture from an abstract idea and turn it into a measurable business discipline. We've already explored some of the sociological and psychological dynamics that have shaped workplace performance over the years. In a moment we'll lay out a step-by-step system for creating and sustaining a strong culture. But first, there are several practical considerations about culture that are important to emphasize.

The first thing to recognize about culture as an organizational discipline is that it happens whether you're intentional about it or not. That wasn't really the case with its predecessors, management and leadership. Without an effort to manage, things don't really get managed. And unless someone applies the principles of leadership, nothing gets led either. Culture, however, just sort of happens whether you set out to create it or not. It's paradoxical. The most powerful of the three organizational disciplines will have a mind of its own if you let it.

The question is how do you *make* culture happen, versus just *letting* it happen? As I've already explained, the best way to leverage this performance-enhancing element is holistically. To help you envision how this can be accomplished, I'd like to present the sequence of events that results in this thing we call culture. There's a common chain reaction taking place in the behavioral spaces where people and work and corporate mission intersect. It's predictable and logical and manageable. Its roots are backed by multiple sciences, including sociology, biology, and of course psychology. But you don't need a deep understanding of those fields to grasp it. Because more than anything, it's intuitive.

The Indirect Discipline

While culture does indeed happen, it doesn't happen the same way other organizational disciplines happen. To manage something in an organization, you simply apply the principles of management directly to the thing that needs managing. To implement leadership, likewise, you identify the people or the initiative where leadership is needed and apply those principles directly. You *lead* them. In that sense, both management and leadership are *direct disciplines*.

Culture, on the other hand, is an *indirect discipline*. This is arguably the most overlooked concept in our thinking about culture. People often assume the way to create culture is simply to *"culture"* it. In other words, to apply culture directly to the thing that needs culture. After all, that's how it works with management or leadership. Therefore, it's common to see companies emblazon the walls with inspiring words and images, or declare the office "pet-friendly," or merely invoke the word "culture" more frequently, and refer to those efforts as cultural initiatives. And while their work is sincere and can often have a positive effect, it's a little like letting a young air traveler "steer" the plane, giving him a set of plastic wings, and declaring him a "junior pilot." It's a superficial gesture that doesn't authentically determine the direction and momentum of the aircraft.

Just because you post your core values on a marble slab in the lobby doesn't mean your culture will automagically line up around them. The "Core Values Speech" popularized by Entrepreneurial Operating System (EOS) is but a nominal enhancement on this impulse. Sure, it's a good start to formalize your intentions, but if you're really going to be the architect of your organization's culture, you'll need to anticipate how the physics of culture behave. Things have mass and volume and velocity and trajectory. And they run into each other and bond and sometimes repel. Your core values are crucial, but culture is not an aspirational utterance as much as it's a by-product of the interactions between a myriad of invisible natural forces.

As organizational disciplines go, the effect of culture work is inherently indirect. That means you must first understand the causality of workplace behaviors and manage the factors that produce them. Furthermore, you should recognize how the various elements of culture interact with each other, sometimes masking or compensating to distort the way culture is perceived throughout the organization. When these dynamics are not taken into account, the C-suite can end up with a perception of the culture that is wildly inaccurate.

Moreover, culture is the result of what happens when people's natural reflexes kick in. The version of culture your customers experience isn't necessarily the carefully-crafted statement repeated in training manuals. It's whatever results from all the complex factors that determine the behaviors of your front-line employees on a given day. It's a combination of their life experiences and their employee experiences. You take whoever they are deep inside and shape it and mold it with training and procedures and environment and send them into the fray. What happens next is anyone's guess. As boxer Mike Tyson famously observed, "Everybody has a plan until they get punched in the mouth."

Life punches people in the mouth every day. *Your* people. They start the day, the quarter, or the year with a picture of how things will go. And invariably, the universe takes its red pen and invokes its authorship upon that picture. When it does, people's reflexes kick in. The fur starts to fly. And whatever was pre-loaded inside your people, just waiting to come out… *that's* what becomes your culture. Indeed, ninety-nine percent of culture is what happens when people get punched in the mouth. It's rarely what was shown in the onboarding video, or orated by the CEO at the annual convention. It's the unfiltered essence of who they are inside. So in order to shape culture, you'll need to operate at the level where human reflexes are formed.

You're not a helpless bystander in this scenario. Yes, people's reflexes can come from deep-seated childhood paradigms. But an ample part of these innate behaviors can be induced by the factors that are within your reach. With a comprehensive framework you can plan and execute an effective strategy to create a culture that amplifies your brand essence on the inside much the way a great advertising campaign does it on the outside. In turn, your culture can establish a competitive advantage for hiring, retention, and performance.

The Purpose of Culture

But inducing those behaviors takes resources and sometimes fortitude. There will be times when more tactical and urgent needs seem to take precedence over investments that take longer to pay dividends. To do it right, culture work requires a strategic commitment to a long-term vision. The company should develop a conviction for being concerned with culture in the first place. As an employee, it's easy to make the case for culture. It makes you feel good. It makes work better… easier. It's more enjoyable. But remember, the organization's first responsibility is a fiduciary one. While all the perks of culture are nice, they're not sustainable if they bleed the company dry. No, if we're going to argue for culture… to invest in it… then there needs to be a strong business case for it. If it's going to be an organizational discipline and not just a bonus for the employees or a legacy for the founder to leave behind, we should fully validate its value as a business asset. As we've already established, culture impacts performance in measurable ways. But let's be more specific. What objectives should we embrace that culture can fulfill?

I know of three immediate, tenable, specific reasons for building an exceptional culture:

1. To attract and retain great people
2. To empower performance by fostering a state of "flow"
3. To demonstrate organizational efficacy

Attracting and retaining the best talent has obvious financial value. When your reputation does the recruiting for you, the quality of your people grows and the cost of recruiting shrinks.

Fostering a state of flow has a direct impact on profitability as well as an indirect effect on numerous other factors, like customer satisfaction, operational efficiency, and employee fulfillment.

Organizational efficacy is a key generator of momentum across the entire organization. When excellence is modeled effectively in one dimension of the company, it establishes a precedent for every department, team, and individual. Thus, a culture of excellence… or efficiency… or creativity… or authenticity… becomes the standard by which all work is measured. Remember, what's measured is what's repeated. That alone makes culture an attractive — if not imperative — investment.

Notice that the list above is not comprised of fluffy epithets and aphorisms about the employee experience. Nothing against giving employees added joy, but those are the very signals that tell CFOs you're merely talking about a quick way to free the balance sheet of excess cash. Culture work carries a stigma. In some circles it is perceived as frivolous nonsense… especially by anyone who watches profit margins. And sadly, in many cases, they're right. In the past, the psychology of the employee experience held little relevance to the performance of a company. In today's workforce, culture can be a significant business factor, but you must be prepared to defend it as an essential business strategy.

Further, too many contemporary initiatives that fly the culture banner are little more than one-dimensional make-overs applied to projects that are perceived by many to be elective or superficial. It can even seem like they leverage the word "culture" to bolster credibility and deflect scrutiny. Fractional efforts to shape culture are often noticeably shallow and only serve to call attention to the unaddressed issues that really matter to employees. It can be a breeding ground for cynicism.

Similarly, culture work should not be confused with brand extensions. I know several companies who create amazing aesthetic artifacts designed to transform an architectural space into an environment that expresses the vibe of the brand. Some of these applications focus on feature-rich fixtures that enhance productivity while incorporating brand design elements and colors. Others showcase floor-to-ceiling wall murals framed by a mixture of organic textures to create a sense of authenticity. It's inspiring. It makes you feel something. And yes, it can influence the culture. But it can also foster the notion that culture is little more than another term for decor.

The same is true for other branded artifacts: experiential meeting designs, cinematic corporate videos, trendy employee uniforms, coffee table books that capture the company "story," posters, t-shirts, and even fully-stocked gift shops complete with jewelry, embroidered sweaters, and coffee mugs. And while all these things can be expressions of the brand and its culture, they can inadvertently contribute to the stigma that culture is an expensive adornment, not an essential business discipline that delivers a measurable ROI. But make no mistake, we are living in an age when the culture of an organization can be its core asset or its terminal disease. And I mean that financially.

One study revealed that 92% of executives believe improvements to their culture would raise the value of the company. When you consider the three reasons listed previously, it's easy to understand why. These three factors alone have enormous financial implications. The value of attracting and retaining great people is measured in both direct and indirect costs; the Society for Human Resource Management puts the average cost of filling a position at $4,129 per hire, and that direct cost typically pales in comparison to the indirect cost of onboarding, training, and stabilizing performance. 86% of job applicants research company ratings and reviews to decide where they'll apply. The value of empowering performance and creating a state of flow, as noted previously, has been shown to comprise nearly half of the output generated by workers.

As much as anything, I hope to impress on you the importance of recognizing culture as an essential, comprehensive business discipline, and to make you aware of the prevailing misconceptions — the stigma — that often keeps leaders from acknowledging and leveraging culture as one of the greatest untapped investments available for companies today.

How Engagement Drives Performance

Since culture is an indirect discipline, I need to explain how it functions inside an organization to impact performance, and ultimately, profitability. A significant portion of this book is dedicated to exploring the framework for optimizing employee engagement in the emerging workforce, and it's important to present the rationale for that emphasis. Human behavior does indeed have an impact on profitability. Furthermore, this relationship can and should be quantified as an operational data point for any business whose value proposition is made or lost in the cauldron of human performance. The rationale is rooted in two key principles:

Principle 1: Culture Obeys Gravity

Ever notice how people with shared interests and values have a way of finding each other? Throw a thousand teenagers together in school and within a few days they'll organize themselves into dozens of subgroups according to each person's natural interests and characteristics. At the high school level, cliques can be awkward, divisive, and downright mean. But look past the rough edges for just a moment and appreciate the raw power of this sociological gravity to create alignment and synergy across otherwise disconnected individuals. Remember, it's not like the teachers and administrators have perfected a system for replicating this phenomenon year after year. It just happens. Imagine if companies could harness those same natural tendencies to create alignment around a common mission!

The same dynamic is at work wherever people groups exist - neighborhoods, churches, clubs, cities, and nations. People find each other. They embrace common causes and interests. They combine strengths. And they don't have to be coerced to do any of it.

Great workplaces leverage this natural force to unite their people and amplify their impact. And you can learn to do it too.

Principle 2: Needs are like Moons

To build on the metaphor of gravity, as people orbit around each other and form into clusters and galaxies, they are being organized by subtle forces. Just as the subtle pull of the moon moves our oceans and regulates a clockwork schedule of high and low tides, people's needs drive them into natural groupings and synergies. Teenagers form cliques based on common needs to examine identities and find their way in the world. And it doesn't stop there. People in the workplace are trying to find their way too. And when companies truly understand what their people need, they stand at the threshold of a workplace concept that runs on natural, sustainable forces. Beneath the layers of malaise and disengagement, people are longing to work. They have an inherent need for agency. They were made to belong, to create, and to contribute.

Unfortunately, our conventional view of laborers as glorified beasts of burden has set us up to overlook the true potential of humans as resources. We've inherited a system that not only neglects their natural abilities, but actually suppresses them. With clunky, mechanical approaches to people operations, we bury the human spirit under layers of disconnected policies and procedures and mandates. Instead of unleashing people into their respective callings, we've caged them with awkward routines and short-sighted business objectives. But it doesn't have to be this way.

Just as managers once faced the task of learning how to be leaders, leaders must now learn how to foster culture.

Every individual possesses the equivalent of a personal "culture." We typically use words like "personality" or "demeanor" or "mojo" when referring to a single person. However, the word "culture" is generally understood to be a reference to the collective personality and demeanor — the mojo — that results when a group is formed. There's an element of chemistry as people merge, interact, and blend together.

Once formed, every culture is characterized by one or more centers of gravity. Like the planets in a solar system, the members of a culture tend to revolve around shared points of interest. They gravitate in the direction of the things they hold in common: passions, activities, experiences, pains, challenges, successes, fears, and aspirations. Wherever people share something in common, a spontaneous symbiotic contract is formed. There's an inherent sense of unity. And unity, in turn, is the currency of all culture. Unity is the material substance upon which sociological gravity acts to form communities, to energize teams, or to start movements.

The tidal pull of unity affects each body and determines the orbital patterns.

Now, in the everyday milieu, unity is often mentioned in the context of an effort to reverse disunity. It's a reminder that we all need to get along, to overlook our differences, and to respect each other. So I should probably clarify that I'm not talking about the kind of unity that happens when people *decide* to act neighborly. In the science of sociology and culture, unity is an objective reality that results whenever two people share something in common. It's not a choice. It's a naturally-occurring material. All other things being equal, a natural alliance exists the moment people recognize a mutual objective. And barring some other source of disunity, the alliance will result in a growing alignment of efforts... a symbiosis.

Harnessing the Moon

The nucleus of a company's culture is not its mission, or vision, or values. The nucleus of all company culture will always be the needs of its people. This is what most companies get wrong when they set out to create culture. While it's certainly important to define the aspirational identity of the company, you can't honestly expect it to inspire an hourly employee the way it does the owner who defined it. It's just not realistic.

> "At the invisible center of every strong culture is a set of common needs around which the employees revolve like their sun."

So how do great companies captivate the hearts of their employees and create a backlog of applicants hoping to get in? They do it by meeting the needs of their people. At the invisible center of every strong culture is a set of common needs around which the employees revolve like their sun. Most are completely unaware of it. But it's the true source of their unity and engagement. They work, not because they long to fulfill the company mission, but because by working they can see and feel their deepest needs being met.

They have a need to earn a living. They have a need to establish a professional identity, and a career path that will secure them into the future. They have a need to develop skills and to exercise them for a sense of accomplishment.

In every thriving culture, these are the needs that people share in common. And meeting those needs is at the center of every cultural universe. It's not the company mission. I'm not saying the company mission is meaningless. In fact, it's an important part of the social contract between employer and employee. The employees offer themselves to any company who will meet this set of core needs. And employers offer to meet those needs for employees who will embrace the company mission, pursue its vision, and reflect its values. And at the risk of reducing it to a transactional quid quo pro, human performance works on the basic principles of positive and negative reinforcement. Culture is no exception.

When people come together around their vital needs, and it's the organization that's fulfilling them, it causes a cultural center of gravity to form.

The Hierarchy of Workplace Needs

As you can see, the first domino in the chain of reactions that creates culture can be found in the needs of the people who comprise that culture. What do they want? What do they need so deeply that it shapes their core motivations in life? What are the non-negotiables that outline their mission and direction in life? What inspires them to offer their discretionary effort to the work they've been assigned? Answer these questions accurately and you'll possess a list of ingredients required to build a strong, sustainable workplace culture.

Employees need many things. Some of their needs are obvious both to the employer and the employee. But many are elusive. They're harder to clarify and define. For whatever reason, people are surprisingly unskilled when it comes to putting their finger on the things they want. Sure, they can name the top five or ten... the obvious things. But motivation is fragile and temperamental. It can be distracted by the slightest imbalance between need and provision. So when a tertiary undetected need goes unmet, it wreaks havoc on a person's ability to perform. In the same way that being a little hungry can suddenly make you realize you're cranky, there are needs people encounter in the workplace that alter their moods, their commitment, and their motivation.

This is why Abraham Maslow's Hierarchy of Needs has become so popular. It brings a sense of logic to our impetuous human nature. It takes random, ever-shifting ambitions and reveals the algorithms that operate them. Maslow showed us why a need can be an obsession one minute and forgotten the next. He gave us the ability to anticipate future demand before it actually materializes. He revealed the overall continuum in which our needs exist, and explained how they correlate to the various conditions we experience throughout life. According to Maslow, our circumstances determine the nature of our interests. And when you understand where a person exists along the continuum, you can predict what will effectively engage them with great accuracy.

Some of our workplace needs are physical and practical. Others are emotional or philosophical. The thing about human resources that sets them apart from other kinds is their finicky nature. To function properly, humans require that certain needs are met even if they themselves fail to recognize those needs. This means employers can't count on employees to accurately catalog everything they require in order to function effectively. Many people live their whole lives and never fully recognize or understand their own needs — the ones that influence their decisions and determine their sense of satisfaction. People in the workplace have complex needs which, despite their direct relevance to the well-being of the individual, are virtually invisible to all but the most scrutinizing observer.

Most Leaders Are Guessing

During the Middle Ages, physicians mostly guessed about the origins of diseases. Their theories focused on toxic vapors, evil spirits, and other fantasies. The world of microbiology was invisible to them. Once viruses, bacteria and parasites were discovered, their treatments improved dramatically. Instead of using leeches to remove "bad" blood, or boring holes in the patient's skull to allow evil spirits to escape, they sterilized their equipment, administered vaccines, and treated infections with antibiotics.

For too long, leaders have been guessing about culture. The psychometrics of the workplace have been invisible to them. It's not that ping pong tables and open floor plans are bad ideas. But can they really answer the specific needs of your people?

To master culture, you need a way to identify the myriad needs that shape the motivational orbit of the people in your organization. You need to quantify them and monitor how they're being met. The human needs within an organization are like a chain that turns the machinery. If a link in the chain is compromised, the whole system is affected.

Fortunately, we don't have to guess about these needs. Most of them are embedded in the existing business disciplines that have been established over the years. For example, the field of management was developed specifically to address certain needs of workers following the Industrial Revolution. Management is the system that enabled companies to meet their employees' needs for compensation, for structured environments with clarified expectations for job roles, and for coordination between various entities. Without the practices contained in management, these basic needs could not be met.

When half the workforce walked out of the fields and into the factories, it was solely for the purpose of getting their needs met.

Likewise, the field of leadership came along later to provide for a unique set of workers' needs that emerged in the 20th century. For example, leadership is designed to activate each worker's need to co-author his or her career path. It helps to satisfy the human need to envision the outcome their work will achieve. And it establishes a code of conduct that promotes a sense of dignity and equality for everyone throughout the organization. Leadership itself is a fundamental commitment to serve, protect, and foster the effectiveness of those a person leads — all of which are essential needs in the workplace.

The Motivational Response Index®

When you put them together, management and leadership begin to frame the central needs that drive culture in a workplace. All that's left is to add a way to address the needs associated with self-actualization — specifically the need for significance.

The Motivational Response Index® is the framework I developed to help visualize the way the needs of workers are encountered in today's workplaces. The bottom tier lays out the needs associated with management — basic survival needs. The middle tier covers the needs that arise with the desire for success — needs primarily met through effective leadership. And the top of the pyramid speaks to the techniques used to cultivate significance through Craft, Cause & Community® — a need that has emerged in recent generations.

In the remaining chapters, I'll introduce you to each of the components in the Culture MRI® framework. When you visualize the workforce through this framework, it becomes clear what it takes to engage and lead the culture of your team or organization. Let's take a look at each component in this framework as well as each need that drives engagement and culture in the workforce today.

Reflect:
What's your favorite definition of culture?

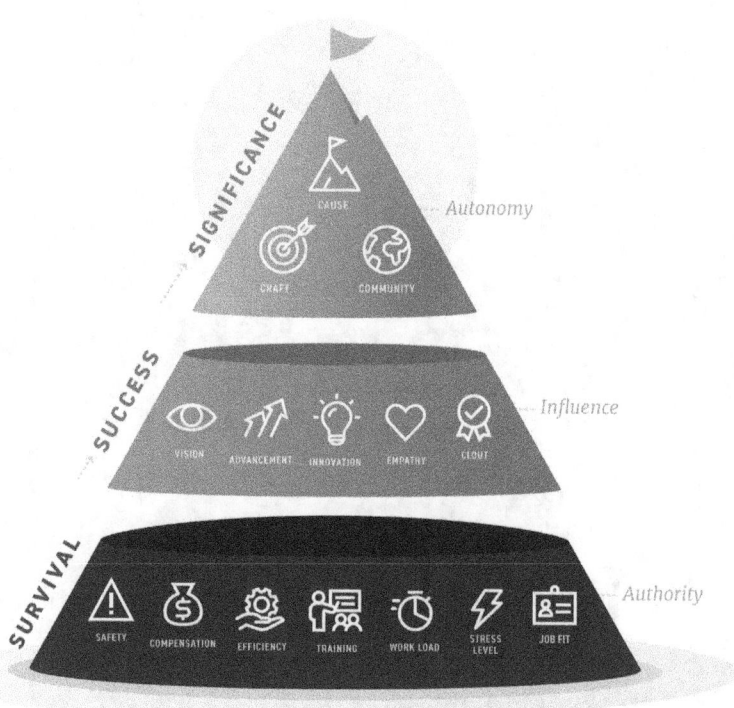

THE MOTIVATIONAL RESPONSE INDEX® (MRI) - THREE LENSES FOR EVALUATING ORGANIZATIONAL CULTURE

In 1962, Maslow spent the summer observing and journaling at Non-Linear Systems (NLS), a manufacturing company in Southern California. His objective was to explore how his theories from psychology would apply in a workplace environment. NLS was struggling with decreasing product demand, and Maslow was invited to examine how the workforce should adapt. Maslow's notes from that summer were later published as "Summer Notes On Social Psychology of Industry and Management" and eventually as the book, "Maslow On Management." Both publications reflect the extemporaneous style in which Maslow originally wrote them, giving readers the sense of sitting alongside the famed psychologist as he scribbled notes on scattered papers in a nonlinear system of his own.

Not long after his time at NLS, Maslow's work began to slow due to health problems. He died only a few years later at the young age of 62. We'll never know the extent to which he would have enlightened the topic of human performance in the workplace. But even in his nascent efforts at NLS, his interest in testing the hierarchy of needs as a lens for understanding worker motivation is evident. Entries in his journal from that summer include, "Different Management Principles at Different Levels in the Hierarchy," and "The Attitude of Self-Actualizing People to Duty, Work, Mission." Maslow had studied the work of Peter Drucker as well as Douglas McGregor's "The Human Side of Enterprise," and he was already aware of the correlation between the levels of the hierarchy in the workplace and the levels of employee motivations associated with each.

In many ways, the Motivational Response Index® is a simplified extension of those theories into the workplace of the 21st Century. Whereas Maslow's hierarchy designated five levels of psychological evolution, mine reduces the workplace down to three: Survival, Success, and Significance®. In my observations, those three categories capture the mindset of most workers. Some are simply trying to survive. Others are focused on achieving incremental levels of success. And still others think of work as an outlet for experiencing significance.

As mentioned earlier, these three levels also correspond directly with the primary operating systems – Management, Leadership, and most recently Culture – that have governed organizations throughout the past century. Management successfully engaged the post-industrial workforce focused on survival, and leadership helped to meet the needs of a workforce in pursuit of the American Dream of success. Culture, as I've posited, should be thought of as a new operating system for millennial organizations whose people are also in pursuit of significance in their work. By 2030, millennials are projected to comprise 75% of the workforce.

The thesis for The Culture MRI® is built on the observation that a company's Employee Value Proposition (EVP) is one of the best ways to evaluate culture. When employees themselves indicate satisfaction with the EVP, we invariably find that the pillars of culture in that organization are also strong. The opposite is also true. Moreover, when we probe into the different psychometrics that comprise their satisfaction, we encounter the very pillars of culture itself. In other words, every culture is the byproduct of complex psychological processes which, when studied and measured, are called psychometrics. Therefore, the psychometrics we record through assessments and interviews give us a direct view into the components of the organization's culture. Adjust those psychometrics and you are moving the knobs and levers of culture. Like flying, it takes some practice to master the take-offs and landings a business can undergo. But the technology awaits anyone with a conviction to learn it.

> *"Adjust those psychometrics and you are moving the knobs and levers of culture."*

The Culture MRI® evaluates culture through three lenses: operations, leadership, and the individual motivations for work. Operations refers to the basic functionality of the company - organizational disciplines drawn primarily from the practices of management. The leadership lens measures the overall *leadership density* throughout the organization - for every contributing employee, there needs to be an adequate distribution of capable leaders to maximize their efforts. The third lens studies the motivational drivers that are unique to each person in the company - namely, Craft, Cause & Community®. Every worker in the world bears a unique combination of these drivers, and in order to sustain a strong EVP with each, companies must offer ways to stimulate each person's unique motivators. Fail to do so and their minds will soon wander, looking for satisfaction elsewhere.

These three lenses are represented as three distinct levels in the Motivational Response Index®. If you're familiar with Maslow's Hierarchy of Needs, you may recognize how these levels are a distillation of the famous framework. They are: The Survival Index®, The Success Index®, and The Significance Index®. By measuring the psychometrics behind each of these organizational layers, we are able to quantify the culture inside it.

The remaining chapters of this book are like a checklist of the elements a leader must cultivate in order to be able to engage employees consistently around the company's objectives, whatever they may be. These are the fifteen disciplines that great leaders employ to meet the motivational needs of their people. Excel at these and you will unleash the natural drive for agency that exists in everyone. Meet these needs and you'll empower a workforce to thrive and produce.

Let's take a closer look at these factors, as well as the psychometrics within each one.

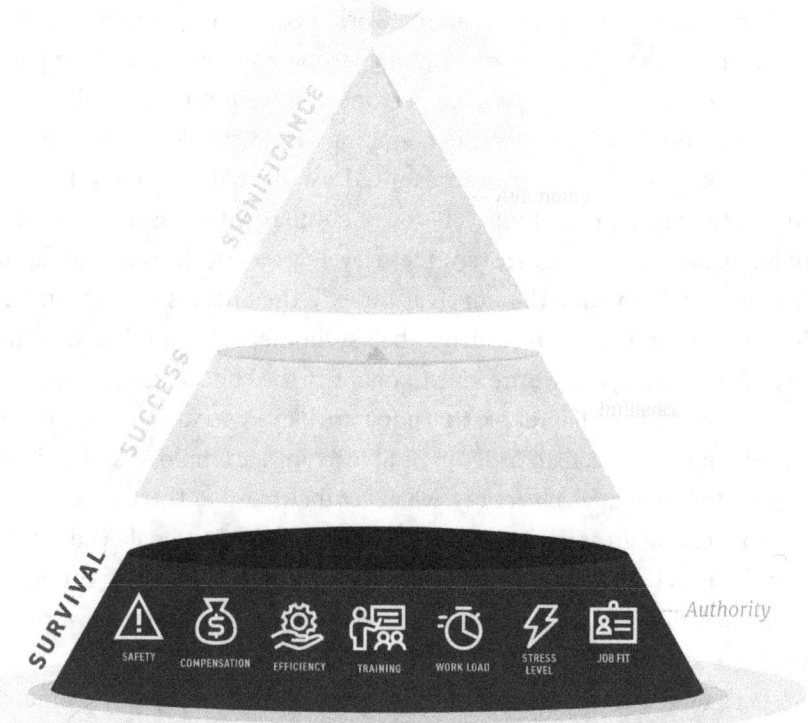

THE SURVIVAL INDEX® - SEVEN PRACTICES FOR MEETING THE SURVIVAL NEEDS AT WORK

Maslow's hierarchy begins with the basics of existence. Similarly, the Survival Index® measures how well the organization meets the most basic needs of the people they employ. There are seven practices from management that are responsible for meeting those needs successfully: the worker's physical and emotional safety, compensation, operational efficiency, work load, stress level, and job fit.

Survival Index® I Authority | Management

The Survival Index® comprises the basic but essential aspects of work satisfaction and security—components that lay a foundation necessary before someone can entertain higher levels of professional fulfillment and achievement.

The Survival Index® is a report card on the company's effectiveness at basic managerial practices. When executed well, they provide balance and stability in the workplace, particularly for those employees whose motivations come from the survival tier of the needs hierarchy.

The field of management was first developed during a time when the dominant motivation of the workforce was survival. Hard pressed for options compared to today's landscape, the playing field between employer and employee was lop-sided. By nature, management bore a style that emphasized authority. It had less to do with catering to the needs of people and more to do with describing what the organization needed from employees. Stripped of perks and incentives, management was developed to provide the basic structure and security necessary for work to continue.

In this chapter, we will explore the survival-level components of the Motivational Response Index® in depth, shedding light on the immense impact of effective management practices. By doing so, we aim to equip you with the insights and tools necessary to guide your team through their survival needs and lead them towards achieving greater heights of professional success.

CHAPTER 5

M1: SAFETY

What would you be willing to do for $50,000?

That question was the premise behind *Fear Factor*, one of the most successful game shows of the 2000s. At its peak, more than 8 million viewers tuned in weekly to see contestants confront their deepest fears and to hear host Joe Rogan issue this chilling disclaimer:

> *"The stunts you're about to see were all designed and supervised by trained professionals. They are extremely dangerous and should not be attempted by anyone, anywhere, anytime."*

The "stunts" Rogan referred to involved things like bungee jumping from a helicopter over a canyon, picking up a live African cave-dwelling spider and eating it whole, sitting in a bathtub full of leeches, being buried alive in a coffin, bobbing for plastic rings in a fifty-gallon tub of cow blood, being locked in the trunk of a car and plunged into a pool, enclosing one's head in a plexiglass container filled with flying insects, and drinking various repulsive concoctions such as donkey urine or a whole, blended rat.

The show begs the question: at what point does fear become a factor that hinders your willingness to do things for money? At the conclusion of each episode, Rogan would declare the winner with the phrase, "You are the Fear Factor champion… and evidently fear is not a factor for you."

One reason for the show's popularity is that everyone considers the same question at some point: what fears would you be willing to face to earn a living? What risk to your safety would you endure?

To some degree, life requires that we overcome certain fears and discomforts to take the next career step. Depending on your *fear factor*, there may be some pursuits that are simply off limits for you. For example, if extreme heights make you cringe, then you'd probably turn down the $19.83 per hour offered to cell tower climbers. Or if the sight of blood, guts, and other bodily fluids makes you squeamish, then you're probably not a candidate for the job of crime scene cleaner, even though it comes with a salary of $33,274. If public speaking terrifies you (this fear, termed glossophobia, is the world's #1 phobia) then you can rule out a host of options, including several that reach well into six or seven figures.

While no job is 100% safe, some jobs are riskier than others. Whether you're a mixed martial arts fighter or a school librarian, every job has its risks. When those risks raise the question of safety, they have a direct impact on engagement, recruiting, and retention. And that makes safety a culture issue.

Statistically, fewer than one in thirty workers will experience physical harm at work. Still, there are legitimate concerns to be addressed. One of our clients is a leading global pizza brand. Pizza has universal appeal. There's an appetite for it anywhere you go. So when this brand opened stores in neighborhoods with high crime rates, some workers actually feared for their lives. There were stores that had been held up at gunpoint. That's enough to make most minimum wage employees clock out and find a different job. To maintain a sense of security in those environments, the company actually created a store design that utilized bullet-proof glass and reinforced doors. Walk-up guests received their pizzas through a slot next to the cashier window. In addition, the company disguised their delivery vehicles to make them blend in with general traffic; apparently, criminals love those lighted signs businesses place on the roof of their delivery vehicles — it helps them identify who's driving around with a pouch full of cash for the taking. We found several stores where turnover hovered near 500%. Store managers would try just about anything to keep people from leaving.

At first glance, safety may seem like a factor that only applies to jobs involving things like heavy equipment, physical labor, or law enforcement. But consider that safety isn't just a physical proposition. It's also a mental and emotional one. Some people don't feel safe because their boss is unpredictably lewd. Others must constantly brace themselves for awkward confrontations with tactless coworkers. Still others feel gaslit by subtle passive-aggressive behavior disguised as courtesies. Let's face it. Some people can be downright mean. When you broaden the definition of safety to include psychological factors like verbal harassment, intimidation, bullying, and corporate trolling, safety can be a very significant part of the equation for organizational culture.

Beyond being entertaining, the show *Fear Factor* proves the hypothesis that fear has a price tag. That's true in your career choices as well as across every organization where employees exist. Safety, then, has a price tag as well. When companies minimize or eliminate fear/safety concerns, they raise the employee value proposition and improve the culture of the organization – which, in turn, drives performance and profitability.

Of course, some people will do anything if the price is right. In the short term, pay raises and bonuses can solve a multitude of problems. But that's no way to manage a labor force. Instead, I'm suggesting that it's much better and cheaper to eliminate the things that compromise workers' sense of well-being in the first place – however large or small they may be. More on this in the next chapter.

I'm also suggesting that very few companies are monitoring these invisible productivity-killers with meaningful data and targeted solutions. That's changing very rapidly. Our understanding of human behavior has progressed by leaps and bounds in recent decades. In the future, human resources will be a sophisticated science incorporating psychometric data that enables companies to optimize the work experience for their people. Human performance is an almost unexplored dimension of the organizational effectiveness matrix. People, once viewed as little more than biologic automatons in the industrial equation, possess vast untapped potential. In the next fifty years, advancements in labor optimization will produce results that rival those produced operationally during the Industrial Revolution.

Remember: the employee value proposition offers one of the most insightful lenses for evaluating culture. Safety is the first of several data points we'll review on the way to envisioning a virtual control panel for monitoring and maintaining a healthy culture. Can you see how something like safety is an important cultural issue? The goal of exploring and measuring each of these components is to be able to prioritize efforts to address culture. If safety concerns are influencing employee retention, you need precise data to understand it. You need to know what it's costing, how to address it, and what the ROI of those investments will be. The end result of this exploration is to gain a comprehensive recognition of the factors that matter to culture, as well as a strategy for focusing your limited resources on the initiatives that will make the most difference to the company's culture and performance. No more guessing!

With today's modern comforts, it's tempting to assume that safety affects only a small minority of jobs and companies. But that's not what the data suggests. In the U.S. 87% of workers struggle with job-related fears, and 81% say it affects their job performance. Most of their anxieties are linked to a general sense of responsibility and the weight of decisions they must make. Many are afraid they'll make mistakes, or be disliked by coworkers, or be fired. And some simply wrestle with traditional phobias like public speaking, large crowds, or social anxiety. As a result, more than a third say they've passed up career opportunities, and many actually miss work. 81% say they'd turn down their dream job if it required them to face their greatest fears.

As Joe Rogan would say, fear is definitely a factor for the vast majority of workers. That's why any assessment of workplace culture starts with measuring fear and safety.

Bullet-Proof Your Culture

Reducing anxiety inside a company starts with an accurate assessment of the things that affect safety. Tracking the overall score is one thing. But the real power comes from analyzing the unique causality behind people's subtle apprehensions.

For most organizations, emotional safety impacts culture more than the threat of physical harm. Even the most sophisticated office environment can't guarantee it's safe to fully trust the people around you. Bullying, cliques, and other subversive behaviors can be classified as integrity issues. When these are present, it's time to work on things like emotional intelligence, leadership density, self-awareness, and interpersonal skills.

To be honest, it's not easy writing those words. Even as I type them, I can feel the same resistance that leads many companies to neglect them. It means pulling away from actual work and spending valuable resources on things that are outside the central mission of the business. I get it. In an ideal world, human resources would always be job-ready, free from defects and sideways energy – thoughtful and well-behaved. For that matter, machinery would never wear out. Taxes would be eliminated. The list goes on.

This is a defining moment in your understanding of culture. Because the instant I mention solutions like soft skills, it triggers a response. There's nothing new about those things. We've tried them all. Perhaps you invest in them regularly. All too often, these gestures have little to no effect. It's frustrating.

So please don't miss the difference this time.

These chapters are not laying out the fifteen things you need to do to build a bullet-proof culture. Instead, I'm recommending a comprehensive system for monitoring the entire culture so that you can identify the healthy tissue from the unhealthy. We call our system the Culture MRI® for a reason. You need a picture of the whole organization – one that gives an unbiased view of what's thriving and what's not. When your heart functions properly, you thank your doctor and carry on with life. If he finds a blockage, you schedule the appropriate procedure and then carry on with life. The same should be true about culture. You should be able to assess what's working and what isn't. Only then can you take responsibility for your culture's ongoing health.

That's what I hope you'll notice as we explore these fifteen concepts. The idea is that when you're armed with accurate data about the factors that really matter to culture, you'll be able to focus limited resources on the initiatives that will make a difference. Every company culture is different. Some are so neglected they could be under investigation by OSHA for troubling safety issues. Others are suffocating in the invisible gas of a toxic leader. And still others are the picture of a thriving, nurturing community. Hopefully, the safety of your workplace will be declared healthy year after year. For most companies we assess, safety is in reasonably good shape. This category rarely represents the biggest opportunity for improving the culture. But like all the elements of culture, safety isn't something you should trust to the naked eye alone. If you don't measure everything, you won't really know your greatest cultural strength from your greatest cultural weakness.

Your organization is like one of the great warships of old. The hull represents your culture. It's designed to be sleek and efficient, absorbing the rolling swells and cutting through breakers. The hull starts out watertight. But the course of battle can leave the hull scarred, cracked, and broken. Water trickles in. Sometimes it pours. These leaks represent cultural imperfections – from small defects that are mostly unnoticeable up to gaping holes where water rushes in. In our metaphor, there are fifteen different seams where water might breach the hull. Each must be examined carefully. The biggest leaks are addressed first. Then the next, and so on.

We call ourselves 'Alcoans'

Safety isn't just about prevention. It can also be a flag to define the culture. When Paul O'Neill assumed the role of Alcoa's CEO in 1987, he pronounced an unexpected priority – worker safety. His declaration bewildered Wall Street, but O'Neill remained steadfast. He held the conviction that safety was the barometer of the company's health. As the safety conditions improved, so too did the company's financial health. By 2000, Alcoa's earnings had multiplied five times over.

O'Neill's focus on safety catalyzed a more engaged workforce, reduced employee turnover, and boosted productivity. It communicated a powerful message to the employees - their welfare was of paramount importance. Alcoa's dedication to safety became their guiding beacon, steering them towards unparalleled success.

Distinguishing Core Values from Core Needs

I'd like to insert an important distinction here before moving on to the next need in the Survival Index®. In the case of Alcoa, Safety was not only a need for the employees under O'Neill's leadership, it was also a core value of the company. There's a difference. A core value is one of the 3-5 intrinsic ideals that defines what the organization is all about. It's a reductive trait that helps to keep everyone focused on the same objective. If you have too many core values, things just get blurry again. For Alcoa, choosing safety as a core value helped to define what the brand was all about. It paints the picture of a company that conducts its mining operations with great responsibility and forethought. It conjures images of an army of engineers and excavators wearing starched white shirts and hardhats, whose systems are not only measured and efficient, they're safe. Internal branding like that goes a long way in helping recruiting, retention, and even customer perception.

I say all this here because I'd like to distinguish the needs in the Motivational Response Index® from core values. The needs in this hierarchy do not represent 15 core *values* that your company needs to adopt. Instead, these represent a checklist of the core *needs* that, if neglected, can erode engagement – gradually chipping away at an employee's ability to stay focused on turning in a solid day's work. Despite its relative importance everywhere, safety might not need to be a core value at a company like GoPro, Atlantic Records, or Rip Curl. At the same time, safety issues can crop up anywhere. And if physical safety even crosses an employee's mind… or if verbal exchanges leave them feeling vulnerable… it can disrupt an otherwise productive, engaged rhythm at work.

Is the threat of crime an issue for any of your people? Are there aspects of the workday that expose them to possible accidents or injury? Are there leaders in the organization whose jokes aren't funny to anyone else?

Physical and emotional safety are important core needs. They might also be core values for the company. So as I describe each of the needs that make up the Motivational Response Index®, keep this distinction in mind. Yes, your organization should do the work of defining its core values. But that doesn't exclude the importance of monitoring how all 15 of these needs are being met throughout the ranks of the organization.

Steps to Consider When Safety Scores are Low

As described above, there are two subcategories to Safety that are quite different from each other. Likewise, the strategies for managing each are also different.

Strategies for Physical Safety will depend entirely on the context of the business. Even if the company is fully compliant with compulsory standards set by OSHA and other governing organizations, it's still important to measure employees' perceptions of physical safety. After all, perception is the dimension that actually influences engagement and performance. Moreover, employees can be a vital source of discovering emerging safety issues that might require additional policies or revisions to existing systems and processes. Things can change. A periodic review of physical safety can avert the need for incident reports down the road.

Depending on the unique ecosystem of your employees, some disciplines to consider might include:

- Independent safety evaluation
    - Lighting
    - Signage
    - Technology
    - Accessibility
    - Employee Ergonomics
    - Transportation
- Independent security audit
    - Facility modifications and safeguards

- Monitoring systems
- Transportation safety
- Time-motion study
  - Workflow safety evaluation and optimization
- Establishing a Safety Committee
  - Internal monitoring
  - Policy and procedure reviews
  - Safety feedback mechanisms
- Safety training audit
  - Compliance confirmation
  - Courseware efficacy
  - Safety data sheets

For additional resources, please visit www.theculturemri.com.

Strategies for emotional safety should focus on resolving threats to employee emotional health and well-being. To address these, you must first be able to identify issues that arise as well as source the causality of the issues. Most of these will fall under these high-level categories: organizational commitment to, and policies regarding, employee well-being; interpersonal skills of leaders and managers; staff selection and onboarding; internal branding and communications; performance management, reviews, and monitoring.

Depending on the unique ecosystem of your employees, some initiatives to consider might include:

- Organizational Development
  - Leadership models and training
  - Leadership programs
  - Core values alignment
  - Internal branding and communication
  - ESG standards and procedures
- Employee Training
  - Management skills and practices

- Sensitivity principles
- Harassment and protocol
- Diversity, equity & inclusion
• Performance monitoring
  - Span-of-control evaluation
  - Workload and stress audit
  - 360 reviews
  - Whistleblower procedures

For additional resources, please visit www.theculturemri.com.

Reflect:
Describe a time when you felt unsafe at work.

CHAPTER 6

M2: COMPENSATION

The television show Fear Factor is not only an experiment in fear; it also serves to demonstrate the central role money plays in fueling motivation. The previous chapter explored the question, "What would you be willing to do for $50,000?" This chapter explores the same question from the opposite end: "How much would it take for you to willingly do _____?" (Insert any job description into the blank.)

While this is essentially the same query run backwards, there are important nuances to notice. In many ways, money is a proxy for all the other elements of the Motivational Response Index®. It's a placeholder. Since money can be traded for virtually any other element of value, compensation is a sort of universal yardstick.

But don't be fooled by that simplistic observation.

Compensation is, paradoxically, the most familiar and the least understood of these fifteen culture indicators. Only a few generations ago, pay was the penultimate indicator of employee value, and therefore the greatest determiner of engagement and performance. If one job paid $8.25 an hour and another paid $8.15 an hour, the former was indisputably better than the latter. Just do the math, right? Count the money. If you wanted to know which job was better than the others, all you had to do was compare the numbers.

More studies have been conducted on pay than any of the other workplace motivators, with some experiments spanning more than 120 years' worth of data. The results, unfortunately, can be difficult to fathom, even appearing contradictory at times. Our intuition seems to tell us, "The higher the pay, the higher the motivation." However, that conclusion is often inaccurate. Several studies actually suggest that in some cases additional pay was determined to be demotivating and actually reduced productivity as well as job satisfaction. How is that even possible? How could more money cause someone to be less motivated? We'll get to that in a moment.

Another group of studies concludes that when additional pay does increase motivation, it has a much higher impact on productivity than all the other types of motivators. For this effect to occur, the work tends to be mundane and otherwise devoid of meaning for the worker apart from the compensation he or she will receive. In that case, more is definitely better.

Finally, if you follow the literature about millennial workers, you've probably heard that they aren't motivated by money. That too might be an oversimplified statement. Again, the key seems to lie in whether other enticements can be found in the work as well. So what are we to conclude about compensation's role in culture? The short answer: it all depends.

Although a pay increase may have a short-term motivational effect, it's almost always a poor device for creating sustained engagement. That's because increases in pay suffer from acclimation syndrome. That is, we get used to them. This is a foundational concept in Maslow's hierarchy of needs. Whenever a need is fulfilled, it quickly becomes the new normal. People forget their past needs with surprising efficiency. As soon as we attain a new level in Maslow's hierarchy, we are introduced to brand new needs and desires. We feel them viscerally too. So much so, that our new needs occupy the space where our former needs reside. There's not room for both. This is why we must be reminded to "practice" gratitude – recounting and reliving the gains we've made and how far we've come to date. So when you pay someone an extra dollar an hour, they soon recalibrate their self-perception of value, concluding that they're worth it. As time goes by, they'll eventually start singing the immortal words of Paula Abdul, "What have you done for me lately?"

Pay Motivates On The Outside

The real key to understanding how compensation impacts engagement is its classification as an extrinsic motivator. Extrinsic refers to an incentive whose impact is limited to a space outside one's personal ethos. Your personal ethos is a set of principles and constructs that form your worldview, your beliefs and values, and therefore they guide your decisions and behaviors. Extrinsic motivators neither fortify nor erode your personal ethos. They're experienced like a benign, emotionless transaction involving currencies whose value is long-since commoditized as a fixed value. To trade in extrinsic tender is to participate in a simple exchange, one asset for another.

Intrinsic motivators, on the other hand, are exchanged on a trading floor that exists inside one's personal ethos. The rules are different in this inner sanctum. Incentives classified as intrinsic directly affect the portfolio of beliefs and values, either adding value or (in the case of disincentives) eroding this sacred treasure. For this reason, intrinsic motivators have the potential to produce an amplified effect. Because they share space with our basic will and intent, intrinsic incentives can be the catalysts behind the most indomitable of human convictions. In other words, when workers exhibit a "do or die" tenacity, it's usually driven by an intrinsic motive such as an important cause or a moral value. Money, on the other hand, is more often associated with bursts of superficial influence.

The net of all this is that increases in pay have the greatest effect on employees who are money-motivated. For those that aren't, money can actually be demotivating. The body of research on this topic concludes that there's an inverse relationship between money and intrinsic motivations. For example, when a worker perceives that the primary value of a task is intrinsic, then only intrinsic rewards are found to be motivating; introducing extrinsic rewards in those situations diminishes the intrinsic value to the worker. It's as if adding money to the equation somehow cheapens the whole proposition and kills the buzz… like the day I found out that waste management companies don't actually process our recyclables. According to some sources, the whole push for recycling is just a marketing facade created to divert our attention from the ever-growing usage of plastics in the packaging industry. Motivation neutralized! Those marketers knew that an intrinsic motivation like saving the planet is much more engaging than giving someone a few extra nickels. Not to mention, it's a lot cheaper. Whether that's true or not, I can't say. What I want you to notice is how quickly an altruistic motive evaporates when it's exposed as a simple money grab.

Bottom line: don't cheapen a priceless ambition by putting a price on it anyway. And don't try to pass off a commoditized task as a lofty quest.

Motivations can vary from person to person and from situation to situation. So it's worth considering which type of motivation is most relevant in each context. Some people are more responsive to transcendent propositions. Others are more pragmatic by nature. Likewise, some initiatives have inherent, transcendent implications, while others represent routine functions.

Your Money's No Good Here

At the height of The Great Resignation of 2021, a national real estate company reached out to our team for help with employee engagement and culture. When we sat down with all the senior leaders to get the backstory, the COO described how their top-performing employees were being poached left and right by competitors. He was proud of their ability to develop people and promote from within. But he explained that the strategy seemed to be backfiring, as now they were preparing employees for careers at other companies.

The head of HR slid a coil-bound report across the table. They'd been using a survey company to measure engagement year-over-year. According to the survey, employees were leaving because they were being offered better pay somewhere else. But I had a feeling that wasn't really the case.

As I thumbed through the pages of the report, the CEO proudly explained how they'd pumped an additional infusion of cash into payroll to give everyone a big raise in hopes of improving retention. It was a LOT of money. I cringed. Looking at the survey data. I could see the engagement scores before the big pay raise, and I could see them after the big pay raise.

The numbers were identical!

I held my breath as I pondered how to tell them that they'd just spent a fortune to patch the wrong hole in the hull of the ship, to borrow the analogy used in the previous chapter. By all indications, they were still taking on water as fast as ever. Had I been able to advise them earlier, I could have shown them the true source of their retention problem. And they could have fixed it for a fraction of what they spent on the raises.

The Necessity of Filthy Lucre

In the portfolio of employee value, compensation is the chief currency... the very purpose for which people work. While the other elements – the ambiance of a positive work environment, the professional development opportunities, or the curated menu of work-life amenities – are essential, they cannot make up for deficiencies in compensation. Neither is money a universal solvent for disengagement.

Put simply, if people come away from the work experience feeling starved financially, you can expect it to hinder organizational effectiveness.

When employees begin to perceive that their work isn't adequately rewarded in monetary terms, a feeling of being undervalued creeps in. The most supportive of company cultures or the most enticing of benefits cannot fill the void left by an inadequately compensated effort. When the balance is off, the harmony dissipates, and workplace culture can see a slump in motivation, a dip in satisfaction, and a rise in turnover.

That being said, I see a lot of companies whose scores seem to indicate compensation issues at first glance. However, money can be the scapegoat for hidden, underlying causes of dissatisfaction. During a period of frantic inflation following the COVID pandemic, a regional insurance brokerage experienced 70% turnover. Similar to the real estate company mentioned earlier, the best managers were leaving for other opportunities, enticed away by a little more money somewhere else. In response, the leaders discussed how to modify the payroll budget to mitigate turnover. To support the evaluation, our firm was brought in to perform the Culture MRI®. Our analysis found that even though employees pointed to pay as the driver of turnover, money wasn't the real culprit. Workers reported procedural issues that were making it unnecessarily difficult to perform everyday tasks. The Culture MRI® analysis projected that an extra $1M in salaries would only result in about $12,000 worth of incremental performance company-wide. In addition, turnover of 70% per year would continue unless the real problem was addressed. Our recommendation, therefore, involved spending less than $100,000 to update certain procedures; the result of which would raise performance and profitability by more than $1M... an ROI better than 10:1. As the old adage goes, "A problem clearly defined is a problem half-solved."

Leaders shouldn't automatically conclude that giving everybody raises will help their culture issues. In reality, people will eagerly accept less pay in exchange for a work situation they can sink their teeth into.

The Dan Price Pay Experiment

For example, consider this real-life study in compensation. Gravity Payments, a credit card processing company, exemplified the power of thoughtful compensation. In 2015, CEO Dan Price made headlines by slashing his own salary from $1.1M to $70K yearly, and increased minimum employee salary to $70K. This move wasn't without controversy or challenges, but the company stood firm on the belief that fair compensation is a key driver of employee satisfaction and productivity.

The results of this experiment have been enlightening. Since the implementation of this policy, Gravity Payments has seen a significant reduction in employee turnover, a boost in productivity, and an increase in overall job applications, thus validating the role compensation plays in motivating people. But you must be careful not to oversimplify it. Compensation is both a tangible metric and a symbolic one, and can be a sign to the workforce that they are valued and respected. As word gets around, the company's reputation for pay will tend to attract precisely the kind of talent it matches out in the pool of potential laborers. In fact, according to Inc.com, Gravity was inundated with résumés – 4,500 in the first week alone. One came from a high-powered 52-year-old Yahoo executive named Tammi Kroll, who was so inspired by Price that she quit her job and in September of 2015 went to work for Gravity at what she insisted would be an 80-85 percent pay cut. "I spent many years chasing the money," she said. "Now I'm looking for something fun and meaningful." In Kroll's case, it was actually the symbolic value of pay that mattered most. Lower pay for senior executives was a way of communicating what the culture was all about.

Whether it's the tangible meaning of competitive pay, or the symbolic way it conveys the values of the organization, pay should be approached with a solid understanding of its role in the overall equation. Pay serves an important need. And you can't expect to understand employee engagement without getting to the bottom of what it means to the employees who make up the culture. In essence, the approach towards compensation must be intentional and thoughtful. Just as a master chef curates a menu that satiates diverse palates, organizations must craft their compensation packages to reflect the value each employee brings. By doing so, they create a workplace environment that doesn't just survive but thrives, attracting and retaining the best talent, akin to a Michelin-starred restaurant that continually draws in and delights its diners.

Steps to Consider When Compensation Scores are Low

As mentioned above, when Compensation scores are low, don't assume you should raise pay. That might not fix the problem... no matter how much you spend! In most cases, pay problems are a sign that something else is wrong. Your primary focus should be to identify the reason(s) pay is perceived as inadequate. Are there other low scores that could be part of a domino effect?

Your strategy should start with causality... what's really behind the issue? Consider these concepts as well:

- Engagement survey (one that shows causality)
- Market compensation analysis
- Employee benefit plan audit
- Career path evaluation
- Personal development plans
- Organizational review
    - Org structure
    - Department alignment
    - Job-leveling

For additional resources, please visit www.theculturemri.com.

Reflect:
Have you ever done something "just for the money"?

CHAPTER 7

M3: EFFICIENCY

Throughout my teens, I enjoyed a rather unusual Thanksgiving Day tradition. My best friend, Stan, was from a family of runners, some of whom were prominent leaders in the Atlanta Track Club. Each year at Thanksgiving, the club put on a marathon race that traversed through the winding streets of suburban Atlanta. As a friend of the family, I was recruited each year to join the family and a handful of other volunteers in laying out 26.2 miles of traffic cones, essentially sectioning off the right lane of each road for the runners. The race began at sunrise, and in the darkness just before the starting gun, our job was to secure the course just ahead of some of the fastest runners in the world. Logistically, it was no small feat. Equipped with radios, bullhorns, and a fleet of small trucks, we timed our placement and retrieval of the orange traffic cones so as to provide maximum safety for the runners with minimal disruption of the city's motorists. The weather might be bitter cold, pouring rain, or both. And even in the mildest weather, Atlanta traffic can be dicey – especially when your job is to reroute it.

Needless to say, hours of preparation went into recruiting, planning, and executing the event each year. Stan's father, Tom, headed up the cone operation. One of his greatest attributes as a leader was the way he empowered the volunteers to help plan the mission each year. Tongue in cheek, he positioned the art of cone logistics as a highly-sophisticated engineering effort. The drivers were precision motorists who could maintain just the right distance from the road's centerline while keeping the vehicle at a steady twenty-two miles per hour. The spotters had a keen eye for keeping the crew alerted to potholes, loose gravel, and other obstacles up ahead. The cone setters possessed the touch of an Olympic curling team, reading the pitch of the road in order to slide each cone perfectly into place on the lane line at even intervals along the course. The goal wasn't merely to clear a lane for the runners, it was to do so with choreographed mastery with each specialist conducting themselves like the professional athletes whose pace threatened to catch up with us if we failed to execute properly. We called ourselves the coneheads.

As you can imagine, the camaraderie of the volunteers spilled over into the offseason. In the months leading up to each marathon, there were ongoing jokes about new techniques and homemade cone-handling machines that promised to inch us ever-closer to cone perfection. And while most of it was obvious sarcasm, it somehow caused us to focus on our respective skills come race day. Putting cones on the road is about as menial a job as there is. But when dressed up with an intricate operational design, it was actually quite fun.

I tell that story to suggest that there's something inside everyone that appreciates a job well done. Moreover, the opportunity to be part of an organization that relies on your mastery for its success – that recognizes it – can be extremely motivating. In a person's everyday job, the operational setting can either feel thoughtful and satisfying, or thoughtless and frustrating. Monitoring the efficiency of operations – the inherent design of each person's tasks inside the overall workflow – is one of the most important steps to understanding an organization's engagement and culture.

Operational efficiency is one of the most influential aspects of culture. A lot of culture efforts deal with improvements to the experiences that are ancillary to actual work, but Efficiency is one that focuses directly on the work itself. From the C-suite, it's easy to lose visibility into the day-to-day workflows of frontline employees. Optimizing efficiency requires getting down in the trenches to find out exactly what it's like to get work done. Is it smooth and satisfying? Or clunky and redundant? There's something inside everyone that longs to be part of a masterful system in which all the moving parts function flawlessly. In contrast, life inside a flawed system is a form of subtle torture that can bleed the life out of even the most committed worker.

If you're going to sustain engagement in the workforce, you'll need to sustain a reasonable level of efficiency for the people who must perform in it day after day. If this element of the engagement formula weakens, the results can be devastating.

Celebrating A Job Well Done

Here's an example from Jones Healthcare, a past client in the nursing industry. This large staffing company had been one of the first to recognize the growing need for in-home caregivers. Right out of the gate they captured a significant share of the market. Business was booming. For the nurses they employed, the job involved conducting rounds from house to house and maintaining accurate medical records in a central database. The company built custom software for the task. Over time, however, things began to change. Managed healthcare was transforming the industry. Insurance regulations and government programs were contributing to a growing list of tedium that accompanied the normal routines of patient care. Nurses whose passion had been to take care of people found themselves working overtime to keep up with all the paperwork. Performance and profitability suffered.

There were other factors too. Dozens of competitors had entered the business. Wages everywhere were rising, putting pressure on the already-tight margins the company ran. Training was also in question since it had originally been designed for a more straightforward nursing role. The leaders pondered how to address the situation. Would additional regional managers help to tighten up their ranks? Was additional training needed to improve support for all the new administrative responsibilities? Maybe the profile of hirees required a few modifications? Should they simply keep updating the software to accommodate the stream of changes? Which, if any, of these initiatives would produce a return on the investment needed to undertake it? Was the company simply coming to the end of its heyday?

Methodically, our team began to analyze each of these factors and their effect on engagement, performance, and profitability. Immediately, we discovered an inflection point that represented a huge opportunity for Jones Healthcare. The nurses we interviewed described intense frustration and disappointment brought on by the shift toward administrative work. As expected, our research found that their primary motivations for work revolved around patients, not paperwork. The job they'd signed up to do was no longer enabling them to thrive in their area of giftedness. They still enjoyed interacting with their patients, but almost half their time was spent entering data into complicated medical platforms.

Based on the findings, Jones Healthcare was able to evaluate the ROI of each potential plan under consideration. After considering all options, they set out to replace their entire records management system with a new one. The incremental performance paid for the whole thing in just three months once the transition was complete. The nurses were happy to return to their passion, and the company's profits nearly doubled in the next year.

From Maze to A-mazing

Picture yourself at the entrance, looking in at the twisted and winding paths of a complicated maze. You're tasked with reaching the center, but the maze is convoluted with unexpected twists, dead ends, and even some treacherous quicksand. It's challenging, perplexing, and, more than anything, draining. The potential joy of the journey is consumed by the exhaustive struggle.

Now envision a different scene. The labyrinth is still there, but it's designed differently. The paths are clear, the turns intuitive, the dead ends minimal, and the quicksand—gone. You're given the same task, but this time, the journey is energizing, stimulating, and enjoyable. This is the difference efficiency can make in an organization.

The design of our metaphorical labyrinth mirrors the operations within an organization. When structured with efficiency at its core, it's akin to creating a logical and navigable maze for the employees. The systems, processes, and procedures form the infrastructure of the labyrinth. When they're streamlined and effective, the employees—our maze runners—are empowered to perform their roles without unnecessary hindrance. They're equipped with the right tools, plentiful resources, and robust support.

Efficiency unshackles employees from unnecessary burdens. It removes the quicksand of cumbersome procedures and eliminates the dead ends of redundant tasks. The path is clear for them to focus on their core work and to move swiftly towards their goals.

Traversing this efficient labyrinth becomes an engaging journey. As the maze runners—our employees—navigate this well-structured maze, each task completed and each goal achieved stokes a sense of accomplishment and satisfaction. Their work doesn't just become a job to do, but an engaging quest.

Toyota (Jidoka)

Toyota Motor Corporation is celebrated not just for the vehicles they produce but also for their innovative manufacturing philosophy. The Toyota Production System (TPS), often described as a "lean manufacturing system" or a "Just-in-Time (JIT) system," epitomizes the pursuit of peak efficiency. It stands as an inspirational testament to the power of continuous improvement, and importantly, it aligns perfectly with our exploration of efficiency in the Motivational Response Index®.

Now, what is Jidoka, you may ask? Think of it as a self-policing mechanism. It allows for the detection of abnormalities within the production process and, in response, halts the machinery at hand. It is best described as 'Autonomation', or, in other words, automation with a distinctly human touch.

Jidoka represents a revolutionary advancement in efficiency. Instead of enforcing a rigid separation between human labor and machine work, it bridges the gap. It imparts human wisdom to machines, providing them with the ability to spot errors and respond accordingly. This eliminates the risk of waste generation and defect propagation. In essence, it's a continual striving towards perfection.

The transformation from manual labor to mechanization, and then to automation, and finally to Jidoka, is a testament to the relentless pursuit of efficiency. Under this system, human intervention is reserved for creative and problem-solving endeavors, where it is most effective, while repetitive tasks are left to machines. The result? A boost in production efficiency and a reduction in costs.

Toyota's tale showcases how embracing efficiency isn't a solitary pursuit but a collective endeavor. Each employee plays a critical role, contributing to a vibrant environment of continuous improvement. It's all about the transformative power of efficiency — fueling engagement, stimulating innovation, and forming the bedrock of high-performance.

Steps to Consider when Efficiency Scores are Low

To address problems related to Efficiency, you'll want to thoroughly evaluate the systems, operations, and workflows that affect employees. Are there procedures that create frustration, boredom, hazards, or menial work? Are there any that are demeaning… or simply annoying? I'm not saying you need to pamper your employees, but you need to take an honest look at what it's like to work a day in their shoes. You may discover some easy ways to eliminate hidden obstacles to employee engagement, productivity, and fulfillment. Here are some common initiatives to consider:

- Workplace Optimization audit
- Time/Motion study
- ISO audit(s)
- Technology audit
- Ergonomics assessment

For additional resources, please visit www.theculturemri.com.

Reflect:
Have you ever experienced a job that was just plain fun to do?

CHAPTER 8

M4: TRAINING

The Tour de France has been called the single hardest sporting event in the world. But while it's definitely hard, there's another bike race that many cyclists dread even more. It's called the Unknown Race. Like the Tour de France, it covers hundreds of miles of Europe's most challenging roads and mountain peaks. There's one crucial, intimidating, horrifying difference. As the name suggests, competitors in the Unknown Race have no idea where they're going until just before the starting gun. There's no opportunity to get mentally prepared. No chance to create a race strategy that aligns their individual strengths with the route details. They aren't even sure exactly how far they'll be going!

The unique wrinkle of this bike race highlights the role that certainty plays in performance. Said another way, uncertainty is disorienting and directly handicaps otherwise capable people, keeping them from performing their best. The purpose of training and instruction in any field – whether in a sport or in a business context – is to eliminate uncertainty as much as possible. When companies establish standards and procedures ahead of time, employees can focus on execution. If those standards and procedures haven't been adequately conveyed, the employee must divert executional energy toward establishing the procedures instead.

For many employees, their job is like an Unknown Race. They don't know what's expected of them until the moment they show up for work. Each day begins with no idea where they're going… or how far. It's disorienting, deflating, and emotionally draining. For the organizers of the Unknown

Race, that was their intention… a unique way to test the mettle of the cyclists who compete. For employers who inadvertently subject their people to this experience in the workplace, the uncertainty accelerates worker burnout as well as turnover. Consider these actual statements from a recent Culture MRI® analysis involving facilities managers for a national company:

> "Everything I do I've had to figure out on my own. There's little to no training before they just throw you into the fire."
>
> "If I have questions or need support, there's nobody I can call. I never really get the satisfaction of knowing I've done a good job."
>
> "They're so desperate to fill open jobs, they didn't want to take the time to train us first. I've seen several people quit because of it. And that becomes a vicious cycle with more and more people quitting and adding to the desperation."

Statements like these are common in my line of work. When there are enough of them to mark a trend, it's easy to understand why the organization struggles to keep employees. You shouldn't guess about the magnitude of issues like this. It's important to calculate the overall impact on profitability before modifying or overhauling training.

According to multiple research studies, a person's ability to rehearse a task or activity affects performance, accuracy, employee retention, workplace satisfaction, and even profitability. Research by IBM looked at "Best Performing Organizations" and concluded that 84% of the companies qualifying for this accolade reported receiving the training they needed; whereas only 16% of those in the lowest performing organizations indicated they were adequately trained. A study by Gallup observed that organizations whose strategic objectives include investments in employee training and development report 11% greater profitability than those that don't.

Bottom line: *high-performing people are highly-trained people.*

Every great journey begins with a single step, and in the workplace, that first step is training. To meet the urgencies of the business, however, training is often reduced to an item on a checklist or a battery of compulsory seminars.

The best organizations view training as an ongoing commitment to support the people they send out into the field. It's a map, guiding employees through the complexities of their roles. In an effort to eliminate crippling uncertainties, these companies leverage everything from interactive workshops and immersive online courses to one-on-one mentoring sessions. In all its forms, the essence of training remains the same: a pledge to empower each individual with the knowledge, skills, and abilities they need to be successful.

Training also includes the ongoing support required to equip people in their time of need. Support takes the concept of training and makes it a process, not merely an event. It's a steadfast companion throughout the workplace journey. Support is a gentle nudge or some timely advice when faced with a crossroads. Support can take the form of a mentor sharing words of wisdom, a handbook full of useful guidance, or a team brainstorming session to tackle a complex problem. Essentially, support is the organization extending its hand, helping its people navigate the journey, especially when the terrain gets tough.

Now, imagine what happens when training and support are intertwined, like two strands of DNA. Together, they form the backbone of an organization, instilling employees not just with skills and knowledge, but also the confidence to bring their best selves to their roles. They engage minds, spark passions, and inspire everyone to contribute towards a shared vision of success.

Ritzy Training

A shining example of this synergistic dance between training and support is The Ritz-Carlton, a luxury hotel chain globally recognized, not just for its opulent accommodations, but also for its customer service excellence.

The secret ingredient behind this outstanding service culture? A meticulous and thorough approach to employee training.

Each new member of The Ritz-Carlton family embarks on their journey with a two-day immersion - an orientation program that takes them beyond the routine company introduction. This immersion is a deep dive into the company's culture, mission, and its heart - the 'Gold Standards'. This collection of service values and operational guidelines serves as a compass, guiding every employee in their pursuit of the iconic 'Ritz-Carlton Mystique'.

But the story doesn't end here. The company maintains the momentum through 'Daily Line-Ups' – 15-minute daily sessions in each department designed to reinforce the Gold Standards and share service excellence stories. This everyday ritual creates a rhythm, helping employees not just remember but live the company's values and standards, day in, day out.

The Ritz-Carlton's unwavering commitment to this blend of training and support has reaped rich rewards. The brand has become the embodiment of top-tier customer service, and enjoys numerous accolades and sky-high customer satisfaction scores. It's proof that an investment in building a well-trained and supported team goes beyond boosting employee morale. It's a promise of extraordinary customer experiences and ultimately, the triumphant success of the organization.

Steps to Consider when Training Scores are Low

Training scores reflect how prepared and supported employees feel. In many companies, training has become a rote function… a box that gets checked. Training has long been recognized as a necessary step in the onboarding process. It's not a category companies tend to overlook completely; however, they may not put enough emphasis on the effectiveness of the training. Do trainees feel confident in their skills? Or do they encounter situations where they struggle to recall instructions necessary to execute their job roles?

When employees have questions, do they know where to turn for answers, or do they feel stuck and helpless?

Training can be expensive. Every hour spent training someone is an hour they aren't employed in actual company output. But in order to build culture, you must also evaluate the cost of ineffective or insufficient training. Consider these concepts:

- Outcome-based training audit
- Training needs analysis
- Employee support system
- Mentoring programs
- Micro learning
- In-line training

For additional resources, please visit www.theculturemri.com.

Reflect:
Have you ever been confused, frustrated, or set up for failure because you were under-trained?

CHAPTER 9

M5: WORKLOAD

Several years ago, I was asked to analyze Sugarland Pools, a regional pool management company that was struggling to find lifeguards for the summer season. The company managed hundreds of pools for neighborhoods, clubs, and resorts across the southeast. Lifeguarding is a momentum business. Once a handful of influential kids sign up to be guards, it can become the popular thing to do for the summer.

For several years, Sugarland had struggled with the same pattern. The summer always started off with a full staff of workers. But by mid-July, their ranks would suddenly dwindle. At first, they attributed it to the flighty nature of teenagers. Sugarland added screening criteria to ensure the lifeguards they hired were mature and disciplined, and could follow through with the job. The problem persisted. Next, they offered special bonuses as the season wore on, hoping to incent workers to finish out the summer. The extra perks had little effect. It was a cycle that seemed to repeat itself no matter what they tried. Worst of all, Sugarland had started losing some of their best customers to smaller competitors who promised stronger local roots and better recruiting depth.

When our team evaluated the psychometrics of Sugarland's labor force, it told an interesting story. The company had failed to create elasticity in their labor mix. If they needed 500 lifeguards to man the chairs, they simply hired 500 kids. However, kids take vacations too. So as soon as the first wave of teens headed off to the beach with their respective families, it triggered an avalanche. To fill the short-term gap, Sugarland's solution was to ask the remaining lifeguards to work double-shifts until the others returned from vacation. This made sense from a coverage perspective, but they didn't take overall workload into consideration.

After two weeks of double shifts, twenty percent of the lifeguards concluded they never meant to spend their entire day in a chair; so they'd quit in favor of a part-time job somewhere else. Now instead of 500 lifeguards, Sugarland only had 400 people to cover the schedule. This meant double shifts for even more kids… so another layer of their workforce would drop out in favor of a more leisurely summer. And so on, and so on…. By mid-July, the company would find itself in a crisis, year after year.

The solution was simple. Instead of hiring 500 lifeguards, the next year Sugarland agreed to leverage the opening day momentum and hired 625 kids instead. This meant extra recruiting costs for the company, as well as additional payroll expenses in general. But the long-term impact would prove to be a net gain by the end of summer. More lifeguards meant fewer hours for each employee, but most kids enjoyed the extra free time. In fact, the added scarcity seemed to add an element of exclusivity to the role. Instead of dreading the long hours, kids actually looked forward to their shifts. Then, when some went on vacation, each pool still had plenty of staff to maintain normal shifts.

As a result, morale sky-rocketed. Pool-goers gave stellar reviews on the management of each facility, reporting better cleanliness and friendlier interactions with lifeguards. Sugarland started growing its customer base again, enabling profitability to recover to previous levels.

Workload is similar to the weight an employee carries while climbing the mountain of their work life. Every hour worked, every task undertaken, and every responsibility a person is assigned adds weight to their backpack. Just as with mountaineering, the trick isn't to shed all the weight but to manage it well… to distribute it evenly, to ensure it doesn't overwhelm and lead to fatigue. As a leader, you are the sherpa guiding this expedition, tasked with managing this load effectively.

Workload isn't just about the hours logged in front of a desk. It's about how those hours intersect and blend with the time spent off-duty. It's the delicate dance between duty and leisure, between obligation and rest. When this dance is choreographed well, it fosters a sense of balance and satisfaction, leading to higher employee engagement.

Just Let Me Do My Job

Jason Fried, the Co-Founder and CEO of 37signals, the company behind the project management tool Basecamp, promotes a novel approach to improving productivity in the workplace. He understood that the key to a manageable workload wasn't just in the hours worked, but also in how those hours were distributed. Instead of cramming in a 40-hour week throughout the year, 37signals experimented with a 32-hour workweek during the summer months.

Fried's innovative system, "Summer Hours," disrupts traditional five-day workweek norms. Summer hours are in effect from May 1 through August 31 each year. This model reduces the workweek to just four days. Employees are granted the freedom to select which day they will take off, providing them with consistent three-day weekends.

You see, 37signals didn't just reduce hours, they made strategic changes to their work culture to ensure that work could be done more efficiently in the shortened week. They minimized meetings, encouraged asynchronous communication, and prioritized tasks. The result? They found that their employees were not only happier but also more productive and engaged, proving that less can indeed be more.

Employers hold the compass in managing the delicate balance between work and rest, between engagement and burnout. It's about understanding that the weight of the workload needs to be distributed evenly and that sometimes, lessening the load can pave the way for a more productive, engaged workforce. The story of Basecamp serves as a beacon, guiding organizations towards a more balanced, productive, and engaging future.

Steps to Consider when Workload Scores are Low

As with many of these culture-shaping factors, they overlap and affect each other. In order to raise the scores, it's important to identify the underlying cause or causes first. That being said, when workload scores are low, here are the three most common ways to take action.

The first step I take when I encounter Workload issues is to examine the workflows for each job role. Many times there are bottlenecks in the operational design that cause work to get bogged down or even to stop. As a consequence, employees are often left to put in extra time to complete tasks all because the company's methods were inefficient, antiquated, or poorly designed. Few things are more frustrating to good employees than being forced to pay the price for the short-sighted negligence of their employers. Smooth operational systems can eliminate many workload issues and pave the way for employee loyalty.

Second, some workload issues stem from hiring practices that fail to match the requirements of the job with the needs of the employees. As we just saw with Sugarland, some employees are looking for a lighter work-life balance, while others will take as many hours as you give them. It all depends on their station in life and their goals for the future. Develop accurate profiles of the ideal employees, including their desires for workload.

Third, staffing models can also be used to correct low Workload scores. The Sugarland example again demonstrates how the original labor strategy was leading to breakdowns mid-way through the busy season. Even though the new staffing model was more expensive, it actually recovered and preserved profitability in the long-run.

In summary:

- Typology models for each job role
- Staffing models for levels of operation
- Span-of-control study
- Ethnography report

For additional resources, please visit www.theculturemri.com.

Reflect:
Have you ever felt overworked?

CHAPTER 10

M6: STRESS LEVEL

Stress refers to the degree of psychological stimulation experienced as a result of exposure to one's professional environment. Low stress environments foster low levels of stimulation, while high stress environments are associated with high levels of stimulation. The human response to stress varies according to the intensity and duration of the stimulation and can range from lethargy and boredom on the low end to anxiety and dread on the high end.

In manageable doses, stress can be an important stimulant, helping to achieve a state of focus and performance optimization. Left unmanaged, stress can cause burnout, fatigue, and disengagement.

Picture a blacksmith's forge. The intensity of the flame is capable of transforming solid iron into glowing lava. It can take a simple piece of raw metal and mold it into a variety of useful items. The proper amount of heat also fortifies the metal, making it stronger. However, if the flame blazes too fiercely or for an extended period, it doesn't fortify but weakens, damaging the very substance it was intended to mold. Stress has a similar effect on people in the workplace.

Stress is an intrinsic element of our professional lives, born out of challenges, deadlines, and the weight of consequential decisions. When harnessed and managed effectively, it acts as a motivational catalyst, stimulating engagement and pushing performance to new levels. It drives individuals toward personal growth, compelling them to scale new professional peaks. It transforms work from a mundane task into a thrilling adventure.

However, when stress transforms into an untamed inferno, it poses a threat, not only undermining productivity, but also endangering the mental health of employees. When stimulation turns to overstimulation, it doesn't fortify but weakens. Sustained, unchecked stress can lead to burnout, a state characterized by profound exhaustion, a sense of cynicism, and reduced professional efficacy. It's a mental health concern that's becoming increasingly prevalent in the modern workplace.

Since 1979

Recognizing the profound impact of stress on productivity and overall health, Johnson & Johnson, the multinational corporation, has championed an innovative approach to employee well-being. Originating in 1979, their response was the 'Live for Life' program, a robust initiative offering an array of resources from counseling to fitness facilities, nutrition education, and smoking cessation programs. It was not just an investment in health but also a catalyst for enhanced job satisfaction and productivity. As an outgrowth of Live for Life, the company introduced Johnson & Johnson Health & Wellness which integrates disability management, occupational health, employee assistance, work-life programs, wellness and fitness.

As a leader in the healthcare sector, their commitment to health is not confined to their customers. It permeates their organization, embodying an aspiration to nurture the world's healthiest workforce. A quick glance at their website reveals this commitment clearly, stating that at Johnson & Johnson, they believe that good health is foundational to vibrant lives, thriving communities, and forward progress.

Understanding the intricate link between fiscal stress and overall health, the company has consciously integrated financial wellness programs into their repertoire of benefits. The popularity of these programs among employees underscores their importance in helping to alleviate stress levels, pointing to a key component of effective stress management strategies. Johnson & Johnson showcases an unwavering commitment to mental health. A broad spectrum of services, ranging from complimentary telephone counseling to in-person sessions with mental health professionals, bolsters the mental well-being of their employees and their families. Furthermore, 24/7 access to educational tools help employees navigate and manage stress, depression, and other mental health concerns.

In recent years they adapted their programs to integrate with technology initiatives. The meQuilibrium, or meQ, app is another innovative tool within Johnson & Johnson's wellness suite. Grounded in behavioral psychology, the app serves as a virtual coach, fostering resilience, agility, and productivity. By offering personalized, practical tips, it supports employees in adopting behaviors that promote health and energy, such as practicing mindfulness.

The collective impact of Johnson & Johnson's comprehensive wellness strategies illuminates a path for organizations aiming to manage stress effectively. Their initiatives offer a model, underscoring the role of managing not just productive workforce, but also sustainably healthy workplaces.

Steps to Consider when Stress Level Scores are Low

The Johnson & Johnson example demonstrates a number of initiatives that can counteract job stress. But managing stress isn't the only strategy you should consider. Companies should also make an effort to identify any sources of unnecessary stress and eliminate them.

One of the most common patterns I find in companies is the existence of stress caused by poor management, usually resulting in frustrating procedures and/or long hours. In those situations, it would be disingenuous to tell employees that you're going to invest in ways to help them manage stress! That's like handing someone an ice pack as you punch them in the face. It might seem to some like a good way to resolve the problem, but it's addressing the wrong part of the equation. Anyone on the receiving end of discomfort is first looking to deal with the source of the pain… then the healing can begin.

In the workplace, stress often comes from poorly-designed systems. Management guru Edwards Deming famously quipped, "Every system is perfectly designed to get the results it gets." So when an organizational system produces burned-out employees, Deming might suggest that it was perfectly designed to do so. Furthermore, he might suggest that it's possible to redesign the system so as to produce satisfied, energized employees instead. The point is that your people probably shouldn't be a "consumable" part of system design. If they are, you can expect to face sustained issues with turnover and recruiting.

Automobiles are designed to consume gas, oil, tires, and brake pads. That aspect of the design enables other parts to last longer. Remarkably, that same mentality once drove the role that people were designed to play in many companies. From assembly lines to coal mines, managers relied on infusions of fresh labor to offset the limited life-cycle each person brought to work. Human churn was just a necessary byproduct that enabled higher profits. When organizations value profit above human dignity, their systems will be designed accordingly.

Some jobs are inherently exhausting to the human will. The point of measuring this factor is to ask whether organizational systems can be designed to optimize the employee experience instead of consuming it. Building an attractive employee value proposition is expensive. But so is turnover. And in many cases, the cost-benefit ratio of the former adds up to a net gain for the company.

Stress management programs can be important. But they're also very risky if used to mask underlying issues. I'm a bigger fan of finding a net gain from enhancing the work experience. Mindfulness activities, exercise classes, "zen rooms," and other stress-abatement measures can be great as long as they aren't an ice pack for avoidable bruising somewhere else in the system. Most companies should probably be doing those things anyway.

For this reason, my response to poor stress scores is always focused on revising the systems that have been designed to produce stress in the first place. Things like:

- Ethnography Report
- Workplace Optimization audit

- Time/Motion study
- ISO audit(s)
- Technology audit
- Ergonomics assessment
- Span-of-control analysis
- Training evaluation

For additional resources, please visit www.theculturemri.com.

Reflect:
How do you typically respond to stress?

CHAPTER 11

M7: JOB-FIT

Shaquille O'Neal was built for basketball. At 7'1" and 325 pounds, he was a dominant player in the NBA, winning four championships and being selected for the All-Star game 15 times. Willie Shoemaker was born to race horses. At 4'10" and 91 pounds, his frame helped him rack up more than 8,000 victories in his storied career. I've often pondered what would happen if the two athletes had switched places for a day. Could a thoroughbred racehorse even finish a lap with Shaq on his back? Could Shoemaker get off a single basketball shot without getting knocked into the third row? The two athletes were among the best in the world, in part because they chose a sport that fit their respective body types.

A similar principle plays out every time an employee shows up for work. Some are ideally suited for the tasks they face. And others are destined to be exposed as underperformers, simply because they weren't an ideal fit for the job they were given. The saddest part of this everyday phenomenon is that most people are good at something. But when they're set up for failure from the start, they can end up thinking it's their fault… that they're not valuable… or that they just don't measure up.

Placing people according to their ideal job-fit is the organization's job. You shouldn't count on the job-seeking public to accurately self-select for the jobs that match their skills and interests. Not everyone possesses that self-awareness. It's up to the company to adopt the procedures that ensure Shaq plays basketball and Shoemaker rides in the Derby.

All work requires some ability to adapt to job requirements. But when workers lack the fundamental make-up necessary to achieve success, it's a recipe for disengagement. Job-fit refers to the alignment between a person's skills and passions, and the role they perform within the organization. It's about placing the right people in the right roles, ensuring their talents and aspirations are in sync with the job at hand.

In an orchestra, each musician brings mastery of their instrument to the ensemble's harmonious sound. Place a flutist at the drums and the concert would lose its melody. Likewise, in a workplace, every employee brings their own unique skill set and passions. Placing them in a role that matches their abilities and aspirations creates a symphony of productivity and satisfaction, fostering a resonating work environment that inspires not just individual success, but collective progress.

There are three lenses you should use to ensure people are placed in the correct "seat on the bus," to borrow the popular metaphor from Jim Collins. The three lenses are: typologies, skills, and interests. Skills and interests are external characteristics, meaning you can discover them in an interview process, or through observation on the job. I won't go into those here. Typologies measure the internal characteristics, which might be the most overlooked and most valuable lens for evaluating and predicting a person's work tendencies.

Typologies

Every candidate and employee should be understood according to their hard-wired behaviors; in behavioral psychology, these are known as typological profiles, or typologies. Just as Shaq can't shrink himself down to 91 pounds, no matter how hard he tries, there are certain cognitive and behavioral functions that just come naturally to some people and are a struggle to others. Psychologist Howard Gardner suggested that there are no fewer than nine types of genius in the population. Donald Clifton popularized the idea of "strengths" in the workplace at his company Selection Research Inc., which later acquired Gallup Inc. Robert Quinn and John Rohrbaugh introduced the competing values framework, which observes that people are driven by the combinations of core values they adopt. Each value also has an opposite value, resulting in an infinite number of variations that make up each person's hard-wired behaviors. Unlike personality types, these behavioral tendencies don't change over time, so they give employers a more reliable way to predict an employee's success over the long term.

I often hear leaders refer to employees who "just get it," implying that the others don't. This is a signal to me that they've yet to quantify the typologies that are essential for success in a given role. You might have to dig under the surface to identify the "highest and best use" of each person. But there are many typology scales and metrics from which to choose.

My favorite tools for organizing employees according to job-fit are those that measure the values of multiple behaviors that are essential to workplace performance. Chuck Russell's tool, BestWorkData, creates a behavioral portrait of each employee based on their propensities for behaviors such as organization versus adaptability, collaboration versus competition, extroversion versus introversion, etc. Evaluate the top performers at any job role using this tool and you'll likely see which attributes you need to look for in future candidates. The companies that use Chuck's tools spare themselves years of frustration and underperformance because they're able to quantify the predictable behaviors that exist in every worker. You can tell a Shaq from a Shoemaker without having to guess.

Google Employees

Google's hiring process is as rigorous as it gets, going far beyond assessing technical acumen. Recruiters seek to comprehend a candidate's approach to problem-solving, their cultural alignment, and their fit with Google's lofty mission. Potential employees often undergo several rounds of interviews, each a step in refining the search for the 'right fit.' This intense focus on job-fit has been instrumental to Google's continued success, fostering a workforce that doesn't just work, but innovates, creates, and inspires.

Yet, this process isn't a one-way street. It also serves to allow candidates to gauge their fit with Google. It's a dance of mutual selection, leading to a workforce that is not only highly skilled but intrinsically motivated, united in the shared vision of the company.

Consider for a moment, the journey of a potential Googler. The process begins with introspection, a deep dive into their own skills, passions, and aspirations. It's an exploration of self, an understanding of what fuels their fires, what triggers their creativity, what defines their successes. The goal is not to hire a mere employee but to welcome a 'Googler' - an individual whose unique skills, passions, and perspectives align with Google's DNA.

From self-understanding, candidates journey into the realm of Google, aligning their aspirations and abilities with what Google stands for, offers, and envisions. They're encouraged to delve deeper, explore, and seek that unique intersection of their individuality with the essence of Google. Every step, from the crafting of resumes to the final decision, centers around this singular focus on job-fit.

Google's interview process maintains this focus, assessing not just skills, but the way candidates think, their problem-solving capabilities, their alignment with the role at hand. It's a process of refinement, of filtering, in the relentless pursuit of that perfect fit. And finally, when the stars align, an offer is extended, welcoming not just an employee, but a new voice to their grand symphony.

Job-fit is not merely a component of effective management; it's the beating heart of it. It's about orchestrating a grand symphony where each player contributes their distinct melody, resonating with the grandeur of the organization's vision. In striking the right chord, in aligning skills and passions with roles, employers set the stage for a performance that echoes with the resonant harmony of success and fulfillment. The power of job-fit, the magic of putting the right people in the right roles, isn't just the music of Google; it's the melody that characterizes every organization, whether they do it well or not.

Steps to Consider when Job-fit Scores are Low

As mentioned, 99% of job-fit is accomplished by understanding the hard-wired behaviors that exist in every worker. Skills can be taught. But the fundamental instincts that so often define an employee's value to an organization are driven from deep within. Everyone has a type, or typology. And you owe it to yourself to map every person and every job role accordingly. Some resources to consider:

- BestWorkData
- Clifton Strengths
- Lominger Competency mapping

For additional resources, please visit www.theculturemri.com.

Reflect:
Describe the perfect job for your talents.

Success Index®

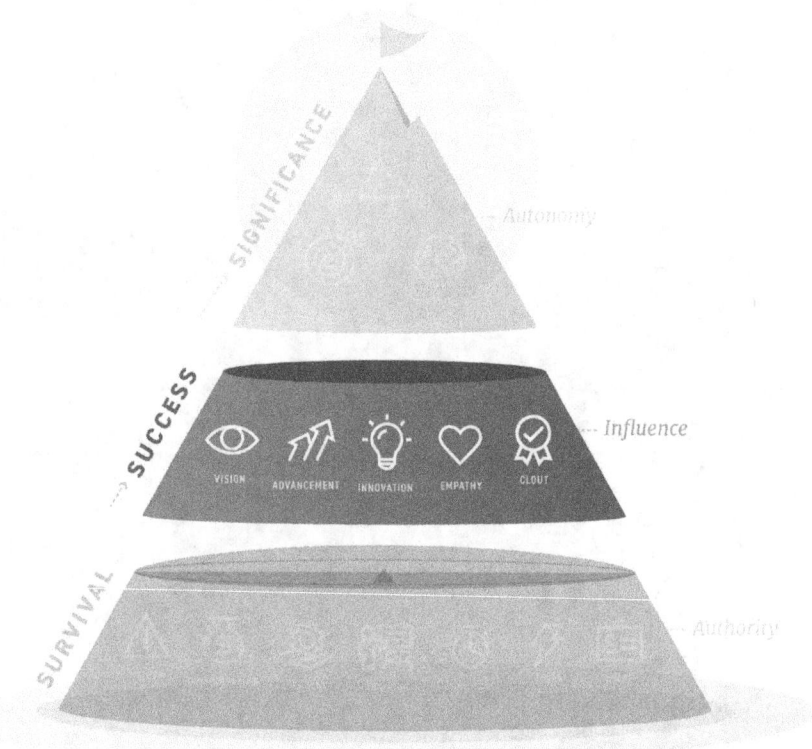

WHO WANTS A MANAGEMENT CULTURE?

We began our exploration of the Survival Index® by situating it within the broader framework of The Culture MRI® and Maslow's hierarchy, emphasizing its foundational role in the workplace. Just as the physiological and safety needs underpin our personal existence, the Survival Index® establishes the fundamental ground on which our professional journey unfolds. Achieve high scores in all seven of these categories and you will have created what might be called a "management culture." If you were born after 1970, that probably sounds like a pejorative term. And for good reason. There was a time when solid management was the goal. It meant you'd covered all the bases. Remember, this lens of The Culture MRI® evaluates the state of general operations across the company. Operations rely on rigid concepts like policies, systems, and standard operating procedures. These are crucial in every organization. However, by themselves they are unable to fully accommodate the more evolved needs of the modern workforce. They're essential, but they're just the starting point.

The social contract in a management culture tends to revolve around authority. When management was first laid out by Drucker and others, the authority of the employer was an important assumption. Managers leaned on their authority to create structure. This social arrangement seems to have been relevant for its time in history. But as we're about to explore, times change, and so must the methods for running an organization.

Even in the modern context, management and authority are often relevant. They create an environment of stability and security, effectively catering to the needs of those employees whose motivation lies predominantly within the survival tier. By employing managerial practices that stress authority, leaders can meet these employees' needs, providing them with the structure they require to feel secure and thrive in the workplace.

Although the Survival Index® has obvious value when measuring manual labor and entry-level jobs, its usefulness doesn't stop there. In addition, it lays the groundwork for further professional growth and advancement. Just as the satisfaction of physiological and safety needs opens the way for us to pursue love, esteem, and self-actualization in our personal lives, the Survival Index® fosters a workplace environment that enables employees to aspire towards and achieve higher levels of professional fulfillment and success.

In essence, the Survival Index® is not just a foundational tier but a continuous supporting structure throughout our professional journey. As leaders, recognizing and addressing this critical aspect of your team members' motivation can greatly enhance their work experience and facilitate their progression along the motivational hierarchy. For additional resources, please visit www.theculturemri.com.

THE SUCCESS INDEX® - THE ART OF INFLUENTIAL LEADERSHIP

The second lens of The Culture MRI® is designed to evaluate the state of leadership throughout the organization. Leadership, when practiced effectively, supports several important components of the Employee Value Proposition (EVP). Therefore, isolating these factors gives us access to the knobs and levers that matter as employees rise through Maslow's categories in their careers. Where the Survival Index® focused on operations, the Success Index® looks at leadership density. As a company grows, it must be embedded with an adequate presence of leaders to sustain the vision, lend support, and ensure performance. When these objectives fall short, it impacts the culture (and the EVP) in very specific ways. The symptoms triggered by these shortfalls indicate which strategies should be adopted to correct culture issues - often before they become visible problems.

Leadership-level components of the Motivational Response Index® represent the key disciplines that come from practicing effective leadership. Credit here goes to Jim Kouzes and Barry Posner. Their *Five Practices of Exemplary Leadership* have emerged as one of the most influential and widely-adopted frameworks for leadership known today. Needless to say, The Success Index® draws significantly on these insights.

Employees experiencing the hierarchical needs associated with success are most responsive to a leadership style that leverages influence rather than authority. In line with Maslow's middle tier—social belonging and esteem—the Success Index® bridges the gap between our fundamental needs and our deepest aspirations. It resonates with our drive to succeed, not merely survive. The Success Index® is not a pit stop on the journey—it's an essential milestone that marks our growth, our strides toward a meaningful contribution, and our unwavering commitment to professional fulfillment.

Success Index® | Influence | Leadership

Just as Maslow's mid-tier is a stepping stone towards self-actualization, the Success Index®, too, acts as a platform propelling us towards higher tiers of satisfaction and achievement in our professional journey. It represents our grounding, yet ambitious endeavors to rise from the basic necessities of the Survival Index® and reach for the profound fulfillment offered by the Significance Index®.

The components of the Success Index—Leadership and Influence—embody the key disciplines arising from effective leadership practices. Much like the esteem and belonging needs in Maslow's hierarchy, these components serve to motivate and inspire employees, particularly those who are navigating the hierarchical needs associated with success.

Employees responsive to the Success Index® are most receptive to a leadership style that emphasizes influence rather than authority. This dynamic shift in leadership approach not only caters to their hierarchical needs but also fosters an environment conducive to their growth and success.

In the next five chapters, we will delve deeper into the Leadership-level components of the Motivational Response Index®, exploring the profound impact of practicing effective leadership. By doing so, we aim to equip you with the necessary tools and insights to guide your team towards achieving greater heights of success.

CHAPTER 12

L1: VISION

This chapter is not about your company's vision statement, as in "mission, *vision*, and values," etc. Instead, I will use the word *vision* here to explore the role mental pictures play in shaping employee motivation. In other words, what do employees picture in their minds when they think about their own work? You may also have a corporate vision and mission statement... and I'm not trying to comment on that practice directly. A corporate vision can be important for setting strategy. But there's another angle to vision that needs its own exploration. When the Board or the CEO sets the corporate vision – even a great one – it may or may not inspire employees. And that's what I want to talk about in this chapter: the broader concept of vision. Your company vision statement might happen to also inspire people... and if so, that's great. But I want to offer some insight into the role that vision itself (again, not your vision statement) plays in creating and sustaining culture.

Vision within an organization is a compelling and aspirational view of the future. It lifts our attention above the mundane tasks and job responsibilities and inspires people to see their work as part of something greater. Peter Drucker, a renowned management thinker, beautifully articulated the concept of vision through the story of three stone-cutters.

In Drucker's tale, a traveler encountered three workers who were all engaged in the same task of cutting stones with a hammer and chisel. When the traveler inquired about their work, their responses reflected their varying perspectives. The first worker replied, "I am making a living," indicating a practical but limited view of his role. The second worker, on the other hand, responded, "I am doing the best job of stone-cutting in the entire country," showcasing a sense of pride and excellence in his craftsmanship.

However, it was the third worker who captured the essence of vision. He paused, looked up at the traveler with a visionary gleam in his eye, and declared, "I am building a cathedral!" Unlike his counterparts, this worker understood that his stone-cutting efforts were not merely about individual tasks or personal success. He recognized his contribution as part of a grander vision—the construction of a magnificent structure that would endure through generations.

Drucker's story powerfully illustrates how vision transcends the immediate job at hand and provides a broader perspective. It involves envisioning the ultimate outcome, connecting individual efforts to a collective purpose, and imbuing work with a sense of meaning and significance.

Don't confuse vision with purpose either. Your vision doesn't have to be transcendent in nature… such as an achievement that saves the world. But it does need to give people a sense that their daily tasks are more than just mundane routines. Their actions are contributing directly to something that matters. I'll share my six attributes for vision in a moment, but for now simply ponder the relationship between what the mind sees and the spirit pursues.

Vision acts as a guiding light that directs the actions and decisions of individuals within an organization. It inspires them to overcome challenges, persevere through setbacks, and strive for excellence in their respective roles. By aligning individual efforts with a shared vision, organizations can harness the motivational power of vision to propel their employees forward.

Vision: The Ultimate Intrinsic Motivator

Aristotle once noted, "The soul never thinks without a picture." In the context of organizational culture and motivation, his statement could be expanded to say, "The heart never engages without a vision." This profound observation highlights the fundamental connection between vision and motivation, emphasizing the crucial role vision plays in inspiring and activating the intrinsic motivations of individuals.

As discussed previously, relying solely on extrinsic motivation is limited in its effectiveness and longevity. External rewards or incentives may initially drive individuals to perform, but their effects are limited. To fully engage employees and foster long-term motivation, it is essential to tap into their intrinsic motivations, which are deeply ingrained within every human being.

Intrinsic motivations revolve around the innate desires for agency, meaning, and social connection. People possess an inherent need to exercise their agency, contribute meaningfully to efforts that hold significance, and to play a role within a social structure. Vision serves as a powerful tool to encapsulate and activate these intrinsic desires.

A compelling vision provides a vivid and inspiring picture of the future. It paints a clear image of the desired outcomes, the positive impact the organization aims to make, and the role that each individual plays in achieving those objectives. When people can envision themselves moving toward these crucial objectives, their intrinsic motivation is ignited.

By communicating and aligning employees with a shared vision, leaders tap into the intrinsic motivations that drive individuals to excel. Employees find a sense of purpose and fulfillment in working towards a common goal that extends beyond personal gain. They feel a connection to something larger than themselves, which energizes their efforts and fuels their commitment.

Furthermore, vision establishes a framework for decision-making and goal-setting. When employees have a clear understanding of the organization's vision, they can align their individual goals with the broader objectives. This alignment fosters a sense of coherence and clarity, unifying personal aspirations with organizational objectives.

Research supports the profound impact of vision on employee motivation. Studies have shown that individuals who feel connected to a compelling vision experience higher levels of engagement, commitment, and job satisfaction. They exhibit greater resilience in the face of challenges and are more likely to persist in pursuing their goals. Vision acts as a beacon that guides and inspires individuals, propelling them towards success.

Vision is Fueled by Communication

Every vision lives or dies by communication. A vision is a lot like a movie poster. It's a visual summary of a larger story. To have meaning, the picture must recall for its audience the full impact of the story. It must remind them of the plot and what's at stake in the outcome. It must stir the same emotions the story evokes. In that sense, a vision is a reference point for a larger story.

Once you've developed your vision, it must be communicated within the organization. This is where companies experience two primary challenges. The first challenge is the tendency of leaders to under-communicate. It is a common human inclination to assume that if something has been said once or twice, it should be heard and understood by others. When a vision makes sense to leaders, they may assume that others perceive it from the same vantage point they enjoy. However, internalizing a vision within a company faces similar obstacles as external marketing efforts.

Even the most compelling vision needs communication to stay alive. Similar to top-of-mind awareness for a well-marketed brand, vision must overcome the existing clutter of information within the organization. It needs to find relevance amidst the myriad of ideas and concepts that employees are already managing. Moreover, it must surpass biases and resistance that hinder understanding and adoption. In many cases, internal communications fall short of the mark, with volume and frequency often less than what is necessary to keep everyone on the same page.

It is crucial to acknowledge that the world around us has become increasingly noisy, while internal communication efforts have often remained the way they've been for decades. Comparing the volume of messages consumed by individuals today to that of fifty years ago highlights the disparity. Internal communications may not have kept pace with the evolving production values, sophistication, and sheer quantity of messages. As a result, the vision risks being drowned out by other competing messages.

To address this challenge, the solution lies in relentless and frequent communication. Companies need to prioritize internal communication and establish a robust communication strategy. It is essential to communicate, reinforce, and reiterate the vision consistently. Just as in marketing campaigns, repetition and persistence are key to ensuring the message cuts through the noise and reaches its intended audience.

The second challenge in communicating a vision sufficiently is that vision tends to fade over time. Merely announcing the vision once is insufficient. Important information requires an ongoing campaign of reinforcements. Mark Miller, who once headed up leadership development at Chick-fil-A, shares a metaphor that demonstrates the nature of vision in a healthy marriage. He says, "You don't get back from your honeymoon and say, 'Honey, I love you. If anything changes, I'll let you know.'" Similarly, sustaining vision in an organization necessitates consistent and deliberate communication — both verbal and nonverbal.

To combat the fading nature of vision, I encourage organizations to think like a media company. This means considering what it takes to establish a significant presence in the minds of constituents. What are the most effective channels to reach employees? What kind of content will it take to break through the clutter that's already surrounding them? And how frequently should you be reinforcing your messaging to sustain the vision and keep everyone on the same page?

By recognizing the challenges of under-communication and the tendency of vision to fade, organizations can proactively address these issues. Robust and frequent communication, along with a sustained campaign of reinforcements, will help anchor the vision firmly within the organization's culture.

Vision Brings Alignment

A strong vision acts as a powerful force that naturally aligns employee goals and values with the organization's objectives. When a vision is communicated adequately, it has a natural aligning effect. It functions like the soundtrack in a movie, setting the tone and helping to move the plot forward. The result is that maximum attention and effort are focused on the company's goals and values. When I see it in action in a company, it's one of the most satisfying sights... as if you're seeing the way people were designed to function all along. I'm reminded of the way a flock containing hundreds of birds swoops and swirls against the evening sky, executing complex maneuvers, moving in perfect sync. An effective vision has the same impact inside an organization.

A compelling vision provides a unifying narrative that transcends individual differences and creates a sense of belonging. It outlines a clear path and purpose that resonates with employees on a personal level. As employees embrace the vision, their individual goals and values become intertwined with the organization's mission. They perceive their work as an integral part of the larger narrative, where their contributions matter and align with the collective effort.

When employees understand and internalize the vision, it becomes a guiding compass for decision-making and prioritization. It helps individuals navigate complexities and make choices that support the overarching goals. This alignment of goals and values brings a sense of coherence and synergy, where employees feel a deep connection to the organization's purpose. They become motivated to invest their talents and efforts towards achieving the shared vision.

Furthermore, an aligned workforce contributes to a positive organizational culture. It fosters collaboration, mutual support, and a sense of camaraderie among employees. The shared commitment to the vision nurtures a cohesive and high-performing team, where individuals work together towards a common destination.

Organizations that successfully align employee goals and values with the organizational vision experience numerous benefits. They enjoy increased productivity, innovation, and engagement among employees. This alignment also enhances employee satisfaction and well-being, as individuals find fulfillment in contributing to a larger cause.

The Six Attributes of an Effective Vision

Sustaining employee motivation over time requires the continuous nurturing and reinforcement of the organizational vision. Developing an engaging vision is a crucial step in this process. To create a vision that resonates with employees, six key attributes must be considered:

1. *Imminent*: The vision should convey a sense of immediacy and relevance. If it's more than two or three years from reality, it gets harder and harder to compete with the concerns of today. The vision should highlight the importance and urgency of the goals and values it represents. By emphasizing the current and future significance of the vision, employees are motivated to take action and contribute to its realization.

2. *Tangible*: An effective vision must be tangible, meaning it should be clear and understandable to employees. It causes them to realize that today's work is connected to the achievement of a desirable outcome somewhere up ahead. It should paint a vivid picture of the future state, making it relatable and easy to grasp. A tangible vision enables employees to visualize and connect with the organization's aspirations.

3. *Mutually-Beneficial*: A compelling vision is one that aligns the interests of both employees and the organization. A vision that involves employees sacrificing themselves to make the shareholders rich is not mutually-beneficial. The vision should bring benefits to employees while also driving the success and sustainability of the company. There are several ways a vision can benefit those who participate in it. Achieving the vision might include growth opportunities, recognition within the industry, or participation in a unique season of camaraderie. When employees perceive the vision as mutually beneficial, their motivation to actively participate and contribute increases.

4. *Realistic*: While a vision should be inspiring and ambitious, it also needs to be grounded in reality. A realistic vision is one that considers the resources, capabilities, and limitations of the organization. It sets attainable goals and outlines a path that is feasible and actionable. When employees perceive the vision as realistic, they are more likely to stay motivated and committed to its achievement.

5. *Measurable*: An effective vision should be measurable, meaning it can be broken down into quantifiable objectives and Key Performance Indicators (KPIs). By providing specific metrics to track progress, employees gain a sense of clarity and direction. Measurability allows for monitoring milestones, celebrating achievements, and making necessary adjustments along the way. The idea here is to eliminate the phenomenon some call "groundhog day," a concept borrowed from the popular movie in which the main character relives the same things day after day.

6. *Audacious*: Sometimes, the best vision is one that requires the best from people. An audacious vision pushes the boundaries of what is perceived as possible. It inspires employees to reach for greatness and surpass their own expectations. An audacious vision challenges individuals to tap into their full potential and fosters a culture of innovation and continuous improvement. It encourages employees to think beyond conventional limits and envision breakthrough achievements.

By incorporating these six attributes into the vision, organizations can develop a powerful and enduring motivational force. A tangible, imminent, mutually-beneficial, realistic, measurable, and audacious vision serves as a guiding star, constantly reminding employees of the purpose and direction they are working towards.

Vision Justifies Tremendous Sacrifice

An effective vision serves as the cornerstone of all employee activity within an organization. It has the power to create and sustain engagement. A compelling vision provides employees with a clear picture of the desired future and the goals the organization aims to achieve. It ignites their intrinsic motivation, inspiring them to go above and beyond in pursuit of the vision's realization. When employees can envision the end result and understand the significance of their contributions, they become deeply engaged and committed to their work.

When an olympic athlete pictures himself winning a medal, he is willing to endure unimaginable obstacles in order to achieve it. That's the power of vision to create and sustain engagement inside the culture of an organization. It fuels employees' dedication and perseverance. A well-communicated organizational vision creates a sense of purpose and direction. It drives people to overcome obstacles, rebound from setbacks, and stay focused on the ultimate goal.

The power of vision lies in its ability to generate and sustain engagement within the organizational culture. It aligns individual efforts, fosters collaboration, and creates a shared sense of purpose. Employees become motivated to invest their time, energy, and talents into the organization's mission, knowing that their contributions play a vital role in achieving the envisioned future.

By embracing vision as a guiding force, organizations can unlock the full potential of their employees. A strong and compelling vision creates an environment where individuals are willing to push boundaries, embrace challenges, and pursue excellence. It fosters a culture of continuous improvement, innovation, and unwavering commitment.

The long-term benefits of a strong vision are far-reaching. Organizations that cultivate and sustain employee motivation through vision enjoy increased productivity, higher levels of employee satisfaction, enhanced teamwork, and improved overall performance. Moreover, a shared vision strengthens the organizational identity, attracts top talent, and creates a positive reputation in the market.

It Doesn't Take a Rocket Scientist

Let's revisit the speech that launched the American space program. When President Kennedy announced the goal of putting a man on the moon, he was modeling how to craft an effective vision. His speech to the large crowd of Americans took place at Rice University in 1962. Kennedy's challenge was phrased like this:

> "I believe that this nation should commit itself to achieving the goal, before this decade is out, of landing a man on the moon and returning him safely to earth."

That one phrase, along with the speech that followed, became a rally point for some of the most important accomplishments of the 20th Century. What followed was a quantum leap in technological achievements, and the solidifying of America as the economic and geo-political leader of the world.

Notice the attributes of vision in Kennedy's simple statement:

First, he declared a deadline for the achievement that felt imminent to listeners. Given the monumental nature of the goal, eight years created a sense of urgency. The timing was important because the Soviet Union was already putting its cosmonauts into orbit around the world, putting fear of Russian takeover into the hearts of many.

Second, the vision was tangible. He didn't say, "We aspire to build a strong space program, enabling America to secure its place in the global landscape." Speeches like that are easy to make. They don't require much conviction. And they aren't very inspiring either. But the moon Kennedy mentioned was literally visible in the sky above his audience at Rice University. That's pretty tangible.

Third, the vision was mutually-beneficial. He wasn't just asking for something *from* Americans, he was calling them to accomplish something *for* Americans. A corporate vision statement doesn't often do that.

Fourth, it seemed realistic. In fact, with Soviet spacecraft passing over the American sky, people were convinced that it was already beginning to happen. There were still plenty of details to work out, but the reality of space travel had arrived.

Fifth, the vision was measurable. We would either land a man on the moon (and return him safely to earth) or not. That's pretty clear. If he comes back dead, it doesn't count. And if it happens in the mid-70s sometime, we might as well start learning Russian.

Sixth, it was audacious. Had Kennedy issued a lesser challenge, would it have been sufficient to capture the imagination of the country? What if he'd said, "*...sending a man into orbit and returning him safely to earth...*"? What if, basically, he'd cast the vision of doing what the Russians had already done? Seems reasonable. After all, we'd never done it before. It would still constitute an important milestone for the country... we'd be keeping up. Instead, he chose something that stretched people's belief in themselves. Theoretically, they knew it was possible... but only if they came together in a special way. It would require something historical in nature... a milestone on the timeline of mankind's greatest accomplishments. And in large part, because of the audacious nature of Kennedy's challenge, it unified the nation around this common goal. Without the element of audacity, the vision would have been, at best, less effective.

Kennedy was no rocket scientist. But it didn't take a rocket scientist to see that an effective vision can be a powerful source of motivation. According to folklore, Kennedy was touring NASA headquarters later that year when he noticed a janitor scurrying past with a mop and bucket. "And what are you doing, sir?" the President asked. "I'm putting a man on the moon, Mr. President!" he replied. The story of the janitor demonstrates what it looks like to work, not for a paycheck, but for a compelling vision that paints a clear picture of the organization's goals.

Steps to Consider when Vision Scores are Low

Vision is like the carrot on the end of the stick. It's the leader's job to keep the carrot fresh. When you go to work day after day, month after month, it's easy to forget about the carrot. When this happens, consider some of the following:

- Create a "man on the moon" vision for your team or organization
- Create a Strategic Plan with visionary outcomes
- Amplify internal communications
    - Channels (Events, broadcasts, trainings, etc.)
    - Modalities (email, video, text, print, etc.)
    - Frequencies (daily, weekly, annual, etc.)

For additional resources, please visit www.theculturemri.com.

Reflect:
Describe a time when vision helped to motivate you.

CHAPTER 13

L2: ADVANCEMENT

As I've mentioned previously, people are born with an intrinsic need for agency... to be engaged in constructive activities. Similarly, we are also imbued with a desire to grow as individuals, advancing our station in life and making progress toward our long-term life goals. When employees sense stagnation in this area, it can severely hinder their ability to fully engage in their work.

According to an IBM study, employees who feel they are unable to grow and reach their career goals within a company are 12 times more likely to leave. According to a 2019 LinkedIn report, 94% of millennials would stay at a company longer if it invested in their career development. This underscores the importance for businesses to build robust employee development programs to keep this generation engaged and committed

In the Motivational Response Index®, a company's success in meeting the need for individual progress is reflected in a category called L2:Advancement.

Much like a well-crafted novel, our employment journey must hold the promise of an exciting arc. A character that remains stagnant from cover to cover hardly makes for an engaging read. In the same vein, a job that offers no scope for growth, no avenues for advancement, is unlikely to spark passion or drive engagement.

Yet, when an organization lays out clear succession paths, it's similar to an author building anticipation, setting the stage for character development. These paths tell a tale of progression, marking milestones, and charting out the trajectory of growth within the company. The clarity they provide is empowering—employees can see where they are headed, understand the strides they need to make, and realize the role they play in the broader narrative of the organization.

This tale of advancement doesn't just serve the individual, though. It creates a powerful loop that drives the organization forward. As employees strive and grow, they cultivate skills, expertise, and leadership potential that, in turn, feeds the success of the company. It's a symbiotic relationship that fosters long-term growth—for the individual and the organization.

In the dynamic landscape of professional growth and organizational success, the concept of 'Advancement' plays a pivotal role. Recognizing the inherent human need for improvement, successful companies offer opportunities for their employees to ascend both in terms of career and skills. Limited advancement prospects, often referred to as a "dead-end job," can trigger disengagement, reduce retention, and incur costs to an organization. This chapter explores how Advancement ensures employees stay motivated and contribute their best efforts to the organization's success.

Fifty years ago, it was entirely reasonable - if not expected - for the relationship between employer and employee to revolve around what the employee can do for the company. The company was only expected to do one thing for the employee: deliver an income. The almighty paycheck entitled an employer to place any number of demands on its workers. "Take it or leave it!" was the essential proposition issued to workers. That mindset is a natural by-product of the management era during which time the social contract between employer and employee was grounded in Authority.

Times have changed. Now the best companies are those that view current employees with an understanding of where they want to be in the future. Companies get the best work from their people when they seek to assist them in moving toward their individual career goals. Sometimes those plans will intersect with openings at the same company, other times they will not. But even if companies must say goodbye in order to help employees fulfill their dreams, there can be tremendous benefits from adopting a mindset of collaborating with employees in their career development, rather than merely thinking in terms of what work they can do today.

How to Approach Employee Advancement

Advancement plays a critical role in maintaining employee motivation and driving organizational success. Career pathing, learning plans, and a culture that supports these can greatly enhance employees' drive and dedication to their work. While obstacles exist, they can be surmounted by a strategic investment in future skills and careful monitoring of program success. By embracing the concept of Advancement, organizations can ensure a motivated workforce that is ready to meet future challenges.

The biggest challenge for many organizations in fostering continuous learning and advancement is a reluctance or inability to invest in their employees' future skills. This can be overcome by recognizing the long-term benefits of such investment, such as increased retention and a ready pipeline of internal talent. The effectiveness of advancement programs can be gauged by monitoring key metrics such as employee engagement, retention, and the number of promotions from within the company.

Career pathing provides a clear route for employees' professional advancement. An employee starting in an entry-level job can climb the career ladder to a senior level position, manager, vice president, and beyond. A classic example is found in the advertising industry, where a worker might start in the mail room, move to a position as a copywriter, and eventually become a creative director or account executive. Designing and implementing such career paths within an organization can significantly enhance employees' motivation and engagement.

A cornerstone of professional advancement is continuous learning and skill improvement. Through learning plans, employees can acquire the knowledge and skills needed to progress in their career paths. Such plans often include formal training, available through the company's Learning Management System (LMS), and informal learning experiences such as coaching and mentoring. Balancing work with continuous learning can be challenging, but companies that manage this effectively reap significant rewards, including higher employee motivation and lower turnover.

Microsoft

Through their well-defined advancement model, Microsoft provides its employees with a clear map for progression. Each promotion, each milestone reached, is like an engaging plot twist, signifying personal and professional growth. The transparency of Microsoft's advancement model empowers its employees, allowing them to visualize their future within the organization, comprehend the steps necessary to achieve their goals, and understand their role in the broader Microsoft story.

However, Microsoft's emphasis on advancement isn't solely for the benefit of its employees. It also serves a strategic purpose for the organization. As employees grow, their expanding skill sets, deepening expertise, and burgeoning leadership abilities feed back into the company, driving its overall success.

This strategic approach creates a powerful feedback loop propelling both individual and organizational growth. The result? A symbiotic relationship where employees grow in step with the company. By investing in its employees' growth, Microsoft ensures a shared journey of success, where every step forward for an individual marks progress for the company as a whole.

In the grand narrative of Microsoft, each employee plays a crucial role. The company's commitment to nurturing this narrative through employee advancement underscores why it remains a global technology powerhouse. It's a potent testament to the transformative power of career advancement, done right.

In sum, advancement isn't merely a corporate policy. It's an unfolding narrative, a tale of growth that satiates the innate human need to progress and evolve. When penned thoughtfully, this story can transform employees into engaged stakeholders and organizations into platforms for growth and innovation.

Steps to Consider when Advancement Scores are Low

The best companies think about Advancement on behalf of their employees, creating an internal system for developing and promoting their people. Consider these concepts:

- Promote From Within
- Personalized Development Plan
- Learning Plan
- Mentoring
- Career Pathing

For additional resources, please visit www.theculturemri.com.

Reflect:
Are you motivated by a future picture you hope to achieve?

CHAPTER 14

L3: INNOVATION

Innovation brings a spark of energy to any organization. It fosters a dynamic environment that keeps employees engaged, motivated, and aligned with the rapidly evolving world around them. Career-minded professionals thrive in workplaces that embrace innovation, as it enables them to remain relevant and competitive in their fields. In this chapter, I'll describe how innovation impacts employee engagement and why it is crucial for organizations to adapt to contemporary practices, technologies, and aesthetics to attract, retain, and engage top talent.

Relevant can mean different things depending on the company and industry. Ultimately, it will be up to you to determine what it takes to remain competitive as an employer in your given field. Does technology matter? Brand identity and aesthetics? Scheduling? Communication? Management style? Identify the factors that matter most to the people in your industry.

In the Motivational Response Index®, a company's success in staying relevant and innovative is reflected in a category called L3:Innovation.

Innovation plays a pivotal role in fostering employee engagement in several ways:

Relevance in a Changing World

Generally speaking, people don't want to work in a place that feels outdated and irrelevant. Sure, there are exceptions, such as a museum or a history center. But even those places strive to show how the things they curate are still relevant to life today. There's something hard-wired into the soul of every worker that responds to current reality. The earth moves through time and space in three discernable dimensions: we are aware of our past, our present, and our future. When it comes to motivation, people tend to engage most with the present. To put it bluntly, we live for the here and now. We appreciate the past, and we learn from it. Similarly, we look forward to the future, as long as it's not too far off. And I'm not saying those other dimensions aren't motivating at all. It's just that most people dance the hardest to the music that's playing right now... the music they can hear. They find the most inspiration and energy from the world they can see and feel around them.

So you can imagine, if they go to work in a place that's frozen in time, it can have a negative impact on engagement. It can feel a little like repeating a class in summer school while the rest of the world moves on.

I'm sure it takes very little convincing for people to understand this point. It's somewhat obvious. However, what's easy to miss is the subtle passing of time and the way it can sneak up on a company, leaving it suddenly in the past. One day you're at the forefront of innovation. You've brought fresh thinking and implemented new ideas. Operations are humming. People are excited. The whole industry is watching, yearning to draw inspiration from your methods. But in what seems like the blink of an eye, the day will come when everyone else has caught up again... possibly surpassing you.

The world around us is continuously evolving, with advancements in technology, industry practices, and consumer preferences occurring at a rapid pace. To remain engaged, employees need to feel that their organization is on the cutting edge, adapting to change and embracing new opportunities. Innovation is not just a project or an iterative upgrade. It's a way of life. A mindset. In the most desired organizations, there's an essence of continuous relevance baked deep into the culture. They don't just play leapfrog, occasionally updating when the carpet starts to look worn. They're constantly thinking ahead, anticipating the world to come, and creating their own future in light of it.

To be clear, I'm not just talking about a campus makeover. Office design, furniture, and communications are important. But innovation encompasses everything the company is and everything it does – from board make-up and operations to brand positioning and talent strategy. Innovation is a mindset that starts at the top and extends to every fiber of the organization. It conveys to employees and customers alike that they are part of a dynamic, living entity that promises to deliver the best the world offers – today as well as in the future.

Career Growth and Development

Innovation also matters in the sense that it can directly impact the individual's career trajectory. We've already covered Advancement in the previous chapter. But the overlap is worth mentioning here. One of the ways to be innovative is through maintaining a contemporary approach to career pathing, skills training, and personal development. People care about their careers, and they tend to engage when the company joins them in caring about their progress. This, too, requires innovation. Innovative companies provide their employees with opportunities to learn and grow. Employees who have access to training, development programs, and exposure to emerging trends are more likely to be engaged and committed to the organization's success.

A Sense of Purpose

We've referred to purpose in the chapter on Vision; in addition, we'll touch on it even more in the chapter on Cause. However, there's another overlap here that we'd be remiss not to mention. People respond to a mission when it's connected to the here and now. Now, if your organization's purpose truly matters, then it will tend to be truly contemporary. In other words, it's impossible for something to matter without being relevant. There's a law of mutual exclusion that applies. But sometimes organizations can overlook the need to be innovative with their purpose. Organizations that prioritize innovation have a strong sense of purpose and a clear vision for the future. When employees understand and believe in the company's mission, they are more likely to feel motivated and engaged. What problems exist right now that your organization – your people – need to solve? What's at stake if they don't solve them? What's the most current update on your progress toward solving them?

Many companies make the mistake of articulating their purpose and simply leaving it there. They're satisfied that the problem has been described adequately. The shortcoming here is that, over time, even the most compelling purpose can start to feel like "the same old same old." It's groundhog day. Again. Innovation means keeping the purpose – your "why?" – continuously relevant.

Innovation Checklist

Innovative thinking shows up in a number of ways. The main thing to realize is that it's a mindset first and a method second. That being said, following are some of the areas to consider when evaluating for innovation in your organization.

Let's talk about technology first.

Technology is an integral aspect of modern workplaces. Embracing cutting-edge technologies not only enhances productivity and efficiency but also demonstrates an organization's commitment to staying ahead in its industry. Providing employees with state-of-the-art tools and resources empowers them to perform at their best, leading to increased job satisfaction and engagement.

One piece of advice I'd recommend is to think in terms of user stories instead of equipment or software, etc. In other words, focus first on how things are done, then on the role technology could or should play in the equation. Approaching things in this order will help to guard against acquiring tools that don't actually contribute to progress. Maybe you've had the experience of hearing about a new technology being used by another organization, and you automatically start feeling the impulse to acquire it yourself. Maybe they know things you don't. Maybe you'll be left behind. It's tempting to piggy-back off the decision-making process completed by another company. But you shouldn't assume their thinking applies to your situation. As with all technology, it should be selected based on user stories, not on gadgetry. How is this technology essential to operations? How will it support our efforts? Enhance it?

Innovative technologies, such as AI-powered automation, virtual collaboration tools, and data analytics, can revolutionize how employees work, communicate, and make decisions. It can also cost a fortune and end up not being used. So be careful. Innovation is a mindset, technology is a method. Don't pursue the latter until the former is thoroughly examined.

When approached in the proper sequence, fostering a tech-savvy culture encourages employees to think creatively and adapt to new challenges, further fueling engagement.

Next, let's talk about Brand Identity and Aesthetics.

A strong brand identity and appealing aesthetics can significantly impact employee engagement. A well-defined brand identity creates a sense of belonging and pride among employees, as they align themselves with the organization's values and mission. Investing in a visually appealing and modern workspace can also contribute to employee satisfaction, as it creates a positive and inspiring environment.

Innovative companies understand the importance of creating a unique and memorable brand presence that resonates with both employees and customers. This alignment fosters a sense of purpose and cohesion among team members, leading to increased engagement and loyalty.

But innovative doesn't always mean reflecting the latest styles and trends. My father-in-law is a role model to me. Before retiring, he ran Georgia Duck and Cordage Mill, which had been started by his father-in-law back in 1916. The company flourished during the heyday of the textile industry and was part of a network of mills east of Atlanta. However, when the textile industry went into decline during the 1970s, my father-in-law saved the business by adding vulcanized rubber to the fabrics and selling conveyor belting for diamond mines, quarries, and shipping companies like UPS. Talk about innovative!

Here's where it gets interesting. Fueled by that one innovation, the mill continued to thrive throughout the 1980s and 1990s. You'd never know by looking at it. The factory was an eclectic assortment of old buildings, many dating back to the company's founding. The looms looked like museum pieces and were kept in mint condition by one of the mill's oldest employees, a resourceful machinist named Grady Washington. The main office was a simple row house separated from the road by a chain-link fence. The walls inside were covered in wood paneling from a renovation in the 1940s. The executives shared small offices featuring plain metal desks also from a bygone era. Framed diplomas and an aerial photo of the plant hung on the wall. The company's logo was an illustrated duck that wore a cape and stood, legs crossed, with hands on hips. It resembled a campy piece of folk art from a roadside stand.

Visibly, the place was the opposite of innovative. Through a strange, countercultural twist, it worked anyway. Atlanta's growth was exploding, swallowing up the quaint suburban towns like Decatur and Avondale. People in the area grew nostalgic about the fading charm of their communities and began to favor the few surviving throwbacks to its local origins. The whole mill stood like a memorial to two periods of innovation – first as a booming textile plant, then as an unlikely source for the world's largest package delivery company. It was understated and kitschy. It was quietly successful and unapologetically retro. The company seemed to possess a

Midas touch, and donated massive portions of its profits to humanitarian causes. Working there carried an esteem comparable to membership in an exclusive country club. The company could have built a modern headquarters befitting its position as the global player it had become. But that would have betrayed its true essence and identity. No, in this case the best demonstration of its innovative spirit was a kind of retro-aesthetic. By doing virtually nothing to its brand identity and aesthetics it found a vibe that was innovative in its own unique way.

Third, let's talk about Scheduling and Flexibility.

In the wake of the COVID pandemic, plenty has been written about work-from-home and return-to-office, so it's important to cover it here. Actually, work schedules were an important topic even before workplaces shut down and sent employees home. Most leaders recognize the impact on culture of having regular office hours with employees physically present. Nevertheless, the trend toward flexibility has been building for decades, and it can be an essential aspect of innovation that influences employee engagement. In general, as the employee population moves up Maslow's hierarchy of needs toward self-actualization, they find themselves yearning for a work schedule that caters more to the rest of life's activities.

Traditionally, work came first. You got a job and everything else revolved around its demands. Your work dictated where you lived, where your kids went to school, and what time you got up in the morning. But more and more, those things are becoming open for negotiation. Companies need top talent. And sometimes that means being innovative with maternity policies, remote working, and travel interests.

In today's fast-paced world, employees appreciate organizations that offer flexible work arrangements, such as remote work options, flexible hours, or compressed workweeks. Such arrangements allow employees to better manage their work-life balance, leading to higher job satisfaction and reduced burnout.

Innovative companies understand that a one-size-fits-all approach to scheduling is no longer suitable for a diverse workforce. By embracing flexible working practices, organizations can attract and retain top talent while fostering a positive and engaged workforce.

Fourth, Communication can be an area that warrants innovation.

During the post-industrial age of management, it was standard practice to communicate with employees on a need-to-know basis. Managers were more likely to guard information, even when it directly impacted workers. And employees generally avoided asking too many questions. But employers and employees follow a modified social contract today. It's no longer based purely on the authority of the leaders. The operative term today is "influence," meaning that leaders are expected to create mutually-agreeable solutions wherever possible. If they don't, it can chip away at the employee value proposition, eventually leading to retention issues.

Open and transparent communication is a cornerstone of any innovative organization. Employees need to feel informed and included in decision-making processes, as it creates a sense of ownership and accountability. Additionally, providing a platform for employees to share ideas and feedback fosters a culture of innovation, where everyone's input is valued.

Innovative companies prioritize effective communication through various channels, such as regular team meetings, town halls, and digital platforms. This ensures that employees remain engaged, feel heard, and understand their roles in achieving the organization's goals.

Finally, Management and Leadership Styles, themselves, are opportunities for innovation.

Innovation in this category starts at the top. How would employees describe the leadership style where you work? Authoritative? Collaborative?

An organization's leadership and management style play a vital role in driving employee engagement through innovation. Transformational leaders who inspire and empower their teams tend to foster a culture of innovation and continuous improvement.

Innovative leaders encourage a growth mindset, where mistakes are seen as learning opportunities, and creativity is encouraged. This supportive environment allows employees to take calculated risks and explore new ideas, leading to higher levels of engagement and job satisfaction.

Innovation is a cornerstone of employee engagement and organizational success. Companies that embrace innovation by staying relevant, adopting new technologies, nurturing a strong brand identity, offering flexibility, promoting effective communication, and adopting innovative management styles are more likely to attract and retain top talent in their industry.

In the ever-evolving business landscape, organizations must recognize the significance of innovation as a driver of employee engagement. By prioritizing innovation, companies can create a dynamic and engaging work environment where employees feel motivated, inspired, and committed to achieving both personal and organizational goals. Ultimately, the pursuit of innovation not only benefits employees but also positions the organization as a competitive and forward-thinking industry leader.

Steps to Consider when Innovation Scores are Low

Some companies are naturally innovative. For others, innovation means change and disruption that can actually hinder operations and progress. In many organizations, this can foster an overemphasis on maintaining stability. New ideas can seem to threaten everything the people have worked so hard to achieve. It takes objectivity to recognize when stability is crossing the line to stagnation. A low score for innovation could be an indicator that it's time to consider the benefits of fresh thinking. Consider these ideas:

- Establish an Innovation Team to evaluate existing processes
- Highlight success stories in communications to emphasize the return-on-stability
- Adhere to change management principles
- Where appropriate, draft a business transformation strategy

For additional resources, please visit www.theculturemri.com.

Reflect:
How important is innovation to you?

CHAPTER 15

L4: EMPATHY

Years ago, anthropologist Margaret Mead was asked by a student what she considered to be the first sign of civilization in a culture. The student expected Mead to talk about fishhooks or clay pots or grinding stones.

But no. Mead said that the first sign of civilization in an ancient culture was a femur (thighbone) that had been broken and then healed. Mead explained that in the animal kingdom, if you break your leg, you die. You cannot run from danger, get to the river for a drink or hunt for food. You are meat for prowling beasts. No animal survives a broken leg long enough for the bone to heal.

A broken femur that has healed is evidence that someone has taken time to stay with the one who fell, has bound up the wound, has carried the person to safety and has tended the person through recovery. Helping someone else through difficulty is where civilization starts, Mead said.

We are at our best when we serve others.

As we explore the factors that contribute to a vibrant workplace culture, it becomes apparent that there is a key ingredient that often sets successful companies apart: empathy. This chapter delves into the profound significance of empathy in cultivating an environment where employees not only work but thrive.

In the Motivational Response Index®, a company's success in reflecting a sense of empathy is measured in a category called L4:Empathy.

To appreciate empathy's role in the workplace, it's important to understand what it means. Empathy refers to the company's reputation for caring about the well-being of each person as much as they care about what the person can do for the company. Is the company known for creating a nurturing environment? Or is it known for "consuming" workers then spitting out the bones? The connection between employer and employee should be approached like any other relationship. If one side is always taking while the other is always giving, there will be an imbalance.

Picture a traditional balance scale with two pans suspended from a beam centered on a fulcrum. On one side are the contributions made by the employer, on the other side are those made by the employee. In generations past, the paycheck was the primary contribution an employer was expected to make. In return, an employee might be indentured for long days of hard labor, strict oversight, and stern correction. And in generations past, employees were often happy to endure harsh conditions in order to receive pay so they could pay for food, shelter, and clothing. But as the social contract between bosses and workers has evolved, companies are required to contribute additional things, such as respect, dignity, and genuine empathetic care. When these things are not present, workers perceive an imbalance in the relationship.

Empathy refers to the capacity to understand and share the feelings of others. It involves recognizing and acknowledging what it's like to be in another person's situation. When employees feel understood by their employers, and when employers express their understanding with efforts to serve the well-being of employees, it's fuel for engagement. Employees sense they can let down their guard and focus on their work. When employees perceive that their organization genuinely cares about them, they are likely to feel more engaged. Empathy humanizes the workplace, breaking down barriers and fostering a sense of belonging.

Psychologically, an imbalanced relationship represents a significant cognitive burden for an employee. In addition to thinking about their duties, they must also look out for their own well-being. That means constantly monitoring and evaluating whether the company is taking advantage of him or her. In a toxic environment, the work of self-protection can be a full-time job unto itself! As you can imagine, this dynamic fosters a guarded relationship between employees and their employers. They tend to withhold any effort that exceeds the minimum requirement.

But when employees sense their company is actually looking out for them, the opposite occurs. Workers are more willing to give their discretionary effort to the company. They view the social contract as mutually-beneficial. It's a shared community in which their contributions go toward an environment that benefits everyone. Including them.

Empathy is an indicator of leadership density. It suggests that the leaders in the company possess a solid understanding of leadership principles and emotional intelligence. They grasp the natural laws of human behavior and the factors necessary to create a thriving environment.

Empathy can manifest in numerous ways: through open and respectful communication, by recognizing and acknowledging employees' efforts, by understanding and accommodating their needs, and by creating safe spaces for employees to express their feelings and concerns. All these aspects contribute to an empathetic culture where employees feel valued, heard, and understood.

Empathy and Retention: The Bond that Holds

An empathetic culture not only enhances engagement but also plays a significant role in employee retention. A workplace that values empathy is likely to reduce turnover and enhance overall job satisfaction.

Employees are more than just cogs in a machine; they are individuals with unique experiences, hopes, and challenges. When employees believe that their employer understands this and cares for their well-being, they feel a sense of loyalty and commitment. This loyalty often translates to lower turnover rates, as employees are less likely to leave an environment where they feel valued and understood.

Promoting Empathy in the Workplace

How can an organization foster an empathetic culture? Here are a few strategies:

1. *Encourage Open Communication*: Encourage employees to express their feelings and concerns without fear of retribution. This openness creates a sense of mutual respect and understanding.
2. *Prioritize Emotional Intelligence*: Leaders should model empathy by demonstrating emotional intelligence, which involves recognizing and understanding emotions in themselves and others.
3. *Show Appreciation*: Recognize and reward employees for their efforts. This not only makes them feel valued but also reaffirms that their contributions matter.
4. *Develop Active Listening Skills*: Active listening is a crucial aspect of empathy. It's not just about hearing what someone says, but understanding their underlying emotions and perspectives
5. *Practice Inclusivity*: Ensure that all employees feel included and valued, regardless of their race, gender, age, or background.

Empathy is more than just a 'nice-to-have' quality; it's an essential ingredient in a vibrant workplace culture. It's the glue that holds teams together, the driving force that spurs employee engagement, and the tie that retains talent.

Steps to Consider when Empathy Scores are Low

By fostering an empathetic culture, organizations can cultivate a supportive and productive environment that not only enhances job satisfaction but also drives overall business success. Remember, the most significant asset any organization possesses is its people. Understanding them, respecting their experiences, and caring for their needs isn't just good practice; it's the only way to truly thrive in the modern workplace. Consider these ideas:

- Increase leadership development efforts
- Evaluate span-of-control
- Develop a robust recognition program
- Establish feedback loops
- Communicate empathetically

For additional resources, please visit www.theculturemri.com.

Reflect:
How important is empathy to you?

CHAPTER 16

L5: CLOUT

My first boss in advertising was a legend. For years I'd heard his name mentioned as an innovator in the business. He was featured on the cover of magazines. He racked up all the prestigious awards. Every agency he led seemed to attract the most desirable clients, and ad people lined up for a chance to work under his leadership. I was one of them.

When I finally got the chance to work for this renowned figure, I was all in. I hadn't even met the guy, but his aura had enveloped me. To say I was engaged is a massive understatement. I was inspired. Sold out. Fully committed.

My first boss had something called clout.

Clout is best described as "radiated leadership." We often think of leadership as a set of skills that anyone can learn. And that's true. Great leaders check all the boxes. But clout is what happens when a leader's reputation and accomplishments precede him or her.

Many companies who come through The Culture MRI® have great leaders. They're practiced at the skills of leadership and they maintain them consistently. Their mission, vision, and values are up-to-date. Their information channels are well-maintained. And they lead from a mindset of servanthood and personal interest. From a culture perspective, there's a tendency to check the boxes and move on.

But as my first boss showed me, there are ways to supercharge leadership and make it radiate through the organization.

It's one thing when you respect and admire your boss. But when a third-party entity recognizes him or her, their leadership begins to radiate.

There's an interesting proverb in the Bible that says, "A prophet is not without honor except in his own country, among his own relatives, and in his own house." It points to the tendency to take for granted the things that are familiar. And even if you don't take them for granted, it's only natural to wonder how they compare to the rest of the world. Clout is the sense of confirmation that comes from third-party recognition. It's the rest of the country bestowing honor on a prophet so even his relatives can't ignore it. Clout takes the big fish out of the little pond and reveals that it's also impressive in the big pond!

To generate clout for the leaders in a company, our team will often cultivate third-party recognition. Industry awards are a great example of peer-generated validation. Feature stories in trade publications and news outlets also contribute to the impression that your leaders stand out from the crowd. If you're not sure how to prime this pump, you could seek advice from a public relations professional.

Many times, our team will add "published author" to the titles of key leaders in the company. When your boss publishes a book, it can change your whole perception of who you're following. They're no longer just the person in charge, they're a *thought-leader*!

Clout, in its most impactful form, is not merely about the capacity to make decisions or command obedience. It is the amalgamation of a leader's professional reputation, their ability to influence, and the profound respect they command within and outside their organization.

In organizations where leaders wield genuine clout, there is a palpable difference in the atmosphere. Employees are not just engaged; they are inspired. They see in their leaders not just the bearers of mandates, but the embodiment of the organization's values and aspirations. When a leader with clout speaks, their words carry weight not because of the authority behind them, but because of the authenticity and wisdom they reflect.

Such leaders become the fulcrum around which an organization's culture pivots. Their influence extends beyond the confines of their immediate responsibilities, seeping into every facet of the organization's operations. They set the tone, not just through directives, but through their actions, their reactions, and their interactions.

Developing clout as a leader is a nuanced journey. It begins with self-awareness, understanding one's strengths, weaknesses, and the unique value one brings to the table. It involves a consistent demonstration of integrity, where words and actions are in constant alignment. Leaders with clout are also lifelong learners, constantly seeking new knowledge, perspectives, and experiences.

Furthermore, these leaders understand the power of empathy. They connect with their employees not just as workers, but as individuals with aspirations, challenges, and lives outside of work. This connection fosters trust, a crucial ingredient in the cultivation of clout.

The impact of a leader's clout extends beyond motivation. It breeds a culture of excellence, where employees are not just driven to meet expectations but are inspired to exceed them. It fosters innovation, as employees feel empowered to take risks and think outside the box, knowing they have the support of a leader they respect and admire.

Moreover, clout at the leadership level has a cascading effect throughout the organization. It sets a standard for aspiring leaders, creating a blueprint for what effective, inspiring, and respected leadership looks like. This ripple effect ensures the sustainability of the organization's culture, securing its future in an ever-evolving business landscape.

Clout and Authenticity

It can take a lifetime to develop clout, but it can be destroyed in an instant. Therefore, I can't talk about clout without mentioning its accomplice: authenticity. If clout were the checks in a checkbook, then authenticity would be the actual money in the account. We've all met someone whose account was overdrawn.

Authenticity is a characteristic, whether positive or negative, of one's leadership. Authenticity refers to the subjective perception that someone's inner values and character are consistent with his or her projected values and character. In the workplace, authenticity determines an employee's ability to trust the leader. And trust, in turn, regulates an employee's enthusiasm or reticence to expend discretionary effort on behalf of their employer.

Authenticity is a continuum that distinguishes duplicity from honesty.

To Walk and Chew Gum

The real issue with duplicity is that it requires employees to multi-task. When workers perceive that their surroundings cannot be fully trusted, they must now do two jobs at once. The first job is the one for which they were hired. The second is the job of protecting themselves from potential harm.

In an ideal culture, the employer ensures that employees are protected professionally, politically, and emotionally. Workers who sense that their environment is safe are able to "let down their guard" and focus more fully on the work at hand. However, those who must not only work but also protect themselves, are severely encumbered.

Trust is a highly influential factor in workplace satisfaction. The lower the trust, the more guarded employees must be. The higher the trust (and therefore, the less guarded), the more an employee is free to focus on the actual job role.

Threats are a natural part of life. Studies show that most species are designed with a built-in "sentry mechanism" that monitors for danger in unfamiliar situations. The old adage of sleeping with one eye open can be traced to actual incidents of this phenomenon in nature. Unihemispheric sleep is the scientific term in which one half of the brain sleeps while the other stays alert. Many fish sleep with one eye open. Several species of birds rely on this state when migrating. Humans, too, are shown to possess the skill. When sleeping in a new location, studies show that one side of the brain sleeps less-deeply than the other.

So why does this matter? Because multitasking is expensive!

The more diluted an effort, the less effective it becomes. Human energy and mental focus are finite resources. The idea is to keep them as focused as possible. Removing threats and increasing trust is one of the best ways to accomplish this.

One study found that learning to juggle three balls is easier than learning to juggle four. Juggling four is easier than five. And so on.

In baseball statistics, RBR measures the number of runs per base-runner allowed by a pitcher. The idea is that a pitcher with a low RBR is more valuable than one with a high RBR. The very existence of this stat comes from the acknowledgement that pitching is one job, but pitching with a runner on base constitutes two jobs. One is to get the batter out. The other is to keep the runner from advancing.

Two jobs are harder than one.

One of the best word pictures for authenticity comes from the historical account of a leader named Nehemiah. In the year 444 BC, Nehemiah led a construction team to rebuild the city wall around Jerusalem. There was just one problem. Some of the locals were intent on sabotaging the effort. As a result, the construction team began working with their tools in one hand and a weapon in the other.

As you consider your own workplace, have you ever felt the need to "watch your back?"

The psychometric for this category is authenticity. The more authentic the workplace, the more an employee can focus on his or her job role.

Quality Control for Leadership

Leadership is not a suit that one can wear on selected occasions; it is an identity that needs to be owned. For workplace culture to thrive, employees need to feel a sense that the people they're following are of genuine substance - free from hypocrisy.

In fact, their connection with their leaders is directly proportional to the level of their trust in the authenticity of the leader. This connection is nurtured when leaders are seen as being authentic, truly "walking the talk" and not merely posing. Authenticity, in this context, can be described as the consistency between a leader's actions and words, their values and behaviors, their inside and outside. It is the ultimate measure of credibility, trust, and respect.

The Motivational Response Index® scores a company's level of authenticity in a category called L5:Authenticity.

Inside Out Leadership

Leadership is not just about being nice and caring… making life easier for people so they'll like you and follow you… or keeping them enticed so they won't leave for another job. Those things can play a role; however, the first rule of leadership is integrity. To have integrity simply means that something is complete, through and through. The structural integrity of a steel I-beam refers to the outer and inner quality and strength of the steel. Is it free from hidden defects or is there a risk that it possesses flaws that may cause it to fail? Similarly, a leader can appear reliable on the outside; but the real question is whether that leader possesses the same internal substance and integrity to make him or her trustworthy. After all, the worker's entire well-being often hangs in the balance. If the leader is only keeping up appearances of good leadership, the employee is forced to spend additional energy covering for the potential outcomes of this deficit. And that takes energy and engagement directly from the mission of the organization.

For instance, a leader who is known for being demanding and ruthless can be just as inspiring as a gentle leader – as long as he is just as demanding of himself. The consistent focus on a certain standard, for himself as well as others, is a sign of integrity. What you see is what you get. The visible exterior is not covering up some hidden inconsistency or ulterior motive.

If you think about it, there are two ways to view a leader. The external view is the initial impression the leader gives off when you first meet them or review their accomplishments. It's possible for the leader to enhance this view by obscuring certain flaws, shortcuts, or conflicting values. The internal view is the one that shows up much later, once you've had a chance to experience what they're really made of. It takes a hard rain to fully test the integrity of a roof; similarly, you find out the true heart of a leader after seeing him or her pass through the fire. This internal view is the one that employees eventually experience – and it results in their perception of the leader's authenticity.

When the internal and the external view are identical, the leader is perceived as authentic.

One of the strongest sources of employee engagement and retention is the conviction that leaders are genuine. When leaders show their true selves - and are proven to be authentic - it not only humanizes them but also makes them more approachable and trustworthy. It encourages employees to engage more deeply, foster open communication, and feel valued. A leader who possesses clout athentically inspires employees to do the same, creating a vibrant culture of integrity and trust.

However, the path to authentic clout is not an easy one. In an era where the spotlight is continuously on leaders, the pressure to perform and succeed is tremendous. The temptation to take shortcuts, to 'pose' as a leader rather than genuinely being one, can be compelling. It might create an illusion of leadership success in the short term but in the long run, it leads to hypocrisy – the very antithesis of authenticity.

Hypocrisy is when leaders don't practice what they preach, creating a dissonance that can breed distrust and disengagement among employees. It can cripple the organizational culture, causing morale to plummet, productivity to suffer, and retention to decrease. Employees are perceptive; they can see through a façade of authenticity. When the disconnect between a leader's actions and words becomes apparent, it raises doubts about the leader's credibility and the authenticity of the organization's values and culture.

Authenticity is like the final quality control check of leadership. It is what validates and confirms that all other aspects of leadership are indeed composed of the best substance. It serves as the bedrock of solid and effective leadership, and its importance cannot be overstated. When a leader is backed by authentic clout, it promotes transparency, empowers employees, and builds a strong and resilient organizational culture.

Leaders striving for authentic clout must take deliberate and consistent action. They must live out the values they profess, be accountable for their actions, show humility, and demonstrate empathy. They must invite feedback and be open to constructive criticism. They must engage in the hard work of investing in people, demonstrating through their actions that each individual's growth and success matter.

To build sustainable clout, one must be willing to reveal their true self, with all their strengths and vulnerabilities. They must be willing to communicate openly, even when the message is difficult. Clout means possessing the moral authority to lead by example, being true to oneself and one's values, and maintaining consistency in words and deeds.

Steps to Consider when Clout Scores are Low

Clout is like steroids for leadership. It has the ability to supercharge the level of influence leaders generate. When leaders possess authentic clout they foster a culture of trust, respect, and engagement. Authenticated clout gives employees a reason to believe in the leadership and the organization's mission. It inspires others and creates a ripple effect that strengthens the fabric of the organization's culture. When clout is lacking, consider these steps of correction:

- Cultivate third-party recognition
- Develop thought-leaders among your ranks
- Increase leadership development
- Emphasize "Servant Leadership"
- Evaluate span-of-control

For additional resources, please visit www.theculturemri.com.

Reflect:
Have you ever experienced a leader who wasn't authentic? Describe how that impacted your work.

Significance Index®

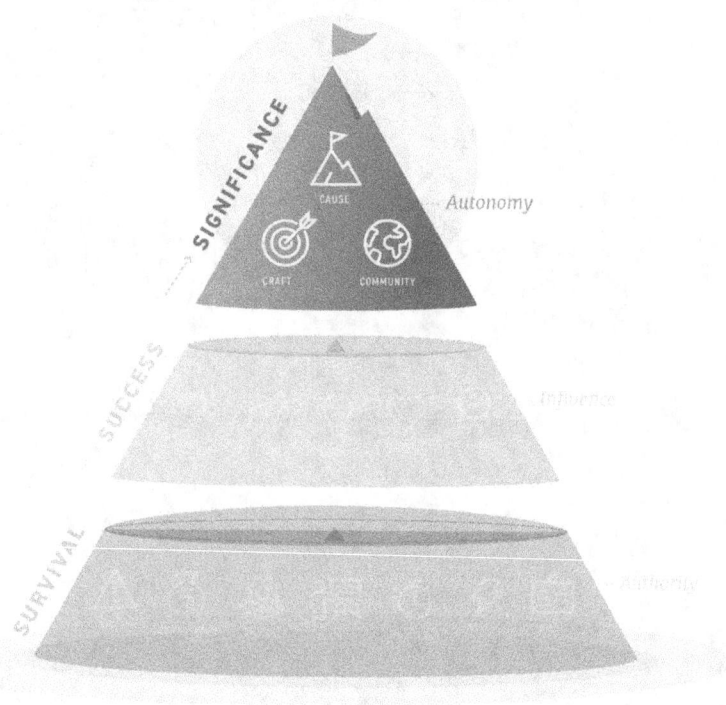

IN SEARCH OF SIGNIFICANCE

The next section will cover the most recent shifts in workplace psychology and how they're rewriting the rules for running a team or a company. As stated earlier in the book, this is the first time in the history of mankind that the majority of the workforce has reached what Abraham Maslow called self-actualization. Fundamentally, today's workers desire something completely unique... unlike anything the previous generations have expected from their jobs. Most notably, this is the first time that a majority of workers are looking to their careers and expecting it to contribute to their sense of significance. Sure, there have always been people who've experienced significance from their work, but in the past that number was small. When the MAJORITY of workers begins to feel this need, it changes everything about the Employee Value Proposition... about attracting and retaining employees... and even organizational structure. The implications on culture are enormous. In this next section, we'll take a deeper look at the inner need that drives behavior and determines engagement in the modern workplace. And we'll explore the three primary motivators through which people express this need and experience significance. In the process, we'll discover a simple grid for understanding millennials and creating a vibrant, productive culture.

The Survival Index® and the Success Index® measure the state of engagement for the social contracts of authority and influence, respectively. In the next section, which explores The Significance Index®, we'll explain why the workforce is changing so dramatically since the arrival of the Millennial Generation.

The influx of millennials into the workforce has introduced significant challenges and opportunities in shaping future workplace cultures. Suddenly, employers are encountering a generation of employees who look to their careers for a sense of significance. Historically, this need has largely been met in other circles of life. One's profession certainly played a role in his or her identity and life trajectory. But for many, work's primary role was provision. It didn't necessarily need to give someone a sense of meaning and purpose. They could experience those things in their religious faith, or through raising a family. Again, this is not to say that all work has traditionally been meaningless; it's just that today's workers almost demand that a job contribute to their sense of significance in life.

This trend isn't going away either. Demographically, millennials are just beginning their dominance of the employment landscape. By 2025, 75% of the global workforce will be made up of millennials. And they're fundamentally redefining organizational norms and expectations.

In addition to significance, younger workers desire the modern conveniences our rapidly-evolving world has taught them to expect. Millennials, also referred to as 'digital natives', rely on technology much more than their predecessors. Deloitte found that 74% of millennials consider technology a major contributor to their work effectiveness. This reflects their desire for a seamlessly integrated, digital workplace. Without it, performance will surely suffer. As such, shaping a future-proof organizational culture will involve creating a tech-driven environment that facilitates collaboration, communication, and productivity.

The traditional 9-to-5 workday is also becoming increasingly less appealing to millennials, 59% of whom value work-life balance, according to a 2020 Gallup report. This generation's drive for flexibility is pushing organizations to reevaluate and adapt their cultures to accommodate more flexible working hours and remote working options. This new emphasis on flexibility will force companies to redefine their culture in a way that supports and nurtures a distributed workforce.

The drive for significance puts emphasis on another key factor that's shaping the future of workplace culture: millennials' commitment to continuous learning and career development. This presents a compelling challenge for organizations to build a culture of continuous learning and development, underpinning their commitment to employee growth and advancement.

However, the real challenge comes in aligning the organization's values with that of the millennials. A Glassdoor survey revealed that 56% of millennials prioritize an organization's culture and values when considering job opportunities. Their focus on environmental sustainability, diversity, inclusion, and social responsibility poses a significant challenge for organizations to reassess and realign their corporate culture. The future of workplace culture will be significantly shaped by how well businesses embody and communicate these values.

After spending four years in a Russian prison camp, author Fyodor Dostoevsky wrote, "If one wanted to crush and destroy a man entirely, to mete out to him the most terrible punishment, all one would have to do would be to make him do work that was completely and utterly devoid of usefulness and meaning." His observation is not lost on today's professionals. The workplace has always been the theater where individuals dance between the need for sustenance and the search for meaning. Today, however, the spotlight shines brighter on the latter, heralding a new age in workplace culture. It's not just about salary, benefits, or job security anymore; it's about significance.

As our workplaces continue to evolve, it's becoming abundantly clear that the age-old paradigms of motivation no longer hold their ground. People's hierarchical needs are changing. Employees are not just looking to fulfill basic requirements, but to attain a higher level of meaning from their professional endeavors. This is where The Significance Index® comes into play, rounding out The Motivational Response Index® and our picture of employee needs.

Significance Index® | Autonomy | Culture

In the earlier sections of this book, we delved into the foundational elements of workplace culture and its transformative journey. Next, we'll explore one of the most groundbreaking shifts in workplace psychology — an era where significance isn't just an aspiration, but an expectation.

Historically, our perception of work was primarily transactional: labor in exchange for monetary compensation. As society progressed, people began seeking more: work-life balance, job satisfaction, and personal growth opportunities. But now, for the first time, we're experiencing a majority of the workforce transcending even these evolved needs. As mentioned earlier, they are reaching for what Abraham Maslow termed as 'self-actualization'. However, in this modern context, self-actualization manifests itself uniquely.

Now, imagine a world where the majority of workers don't just seek a paycheck, but a purpose; not just a job title, but a journey; not merely a position, but a passion. This isn't a future scenario, it's the present reality. And this transformation changes every rule we thought we knew about team management, employee retention, and organizational dynamics. When the majority desires not just to be part of an organization but to find significance within it, it doesn't just modify the Employee Value Proposition (EVP), it reinvents it.

Let's delve deeper.

The Significance Index® segments the modern motivators into three distinct but interrelated pillars: Craft, Cause, and Community®.

Craft speaks to the deep-seated desire of individuals to excel in their chosen field, to continuously hone their skills, and to be recognized for their unique contributions. It's not just about performing a task, but mastering it. It's the internal flame that drives an artist to perfect a piece, or an engineer to refine a blueprint. In a corporate setting, it pertains to the cultivation and appreciation of individual skill sets and talents.

Cause refers to the larger purpose or mission that individuals align themselves with. It's the driving force that propels employees to contribute not just to the organization but to a greater societal or global goal. It's the difference between selling shoes and enabling individuals to walk their path with confidence.

Community centers on the relationships and connections we form in our professional lives. It's about fostering an environment of collaboration, belonging, and mutual respect. It's the camaraderie shared between teammates, the mentorship between senior and junior employees, and the shared purpose that binds an organization.

These are the three expressions through which people experience significance at work. They long to "matter." And that's exactly how they feel when they're good at something (Craft), when they believe in something (Cause), or when they belong to something (Community). Through this section, we'll unravel the intricacies of each motivator, highlighting actionable insights, case studies, and best practices for crafting a workplace that doesn't just function but flourishes.

In the journey ahead, we'll uncover not just what makes the modern worker tick, but how organizations can adapt, innovate, and thrive in this era of significance. Welcome to the future of work, where significance isn't just a pithy mission statement — it's a golden thread throughout the employee experience.

For additional resources, please visit www.theculturemri.com.

CHAPTER 17

C1: CRAFT

My ninth grade philosophy teacher stepped to the lectern and announced the class project for the semester. An audible groan filled the room. Perhaps you remember class projects. You're paired with other students to take an obscure topic and pretend to find something interesting about it. You're given the option of presenting a lecture on your topic, or a slide show, or a skit, etc. When the class dismissed, adolescent boys and girls spilled out into the hallway, shoulders slumped with dread. But not me. I had a plan. In my mind, key moments of the presentation were already appearing like scenes from a thrilling movie. Don't get me wrong, I really struggled scholastically. Sitting still at a desk did not fit my personality at all. I spent so much energy containing my fidgety nature that I had little left for whatever was being taught in the actual lessons. I probably should have been on medication.

Nevertheless, this assignment landed differently. It sent my fidgety mind on a mission like nothing else in academia.

So what was it that awakened engagement in me so markedly? Was it a riveting philosophical question posed by a sage of old? Or perhaps my random pairing with Alan, the one classmate who didn't seem to mind being paired with me? No, it was neither of those things. My enthusiasm owed its origins to an almost unrelated coincidence. During the previous Summer, I'd been introduced to the world of film production at a church retreat. Henry, one of the church youth leaders (and a veteran producer), led a hands-on workshop in which a bunch of us kids wrote, filmed, and edited our own productions. The film bug bit me hard.

Or to put it in terms befitting this chapter, I'd found a Craft to master.

The old saying goes, "When you're a hammer, everything's a nail." That aphorism is usually a pejorative commentary about people's tendency to bulldoze through life with their predictable biases. But it can also mean that each individual brings a unique, valuable perspective to any given situation. In my case, I was a freshly-minted producer, and everything was a potential film to me. So when my philosophy teacher handed out the assignments for the class project, I saw an opportunity to make a movie!

Several weeks later, the day came to give our presentation. With great anticipation, the class marched down to the school auditorium, where I'd set up equipment borrowed from youth leader Henry to show our film about the philosopher Thomas Aquinas. The house lights dimmed. A faint light flickered from the screen as the soundtrack transported the audience back in time. Suddenly, the white light of the cosmos illuminated the building. The room shook.

Ten minutes later, the presentation ended and the class erupted with applause. The teacher was speechless. Even the class bully, in a gesture that almost convinced me he was human, turned to me and said, "That was awesome." I received an A for the project – one of the few I would earn as a high school student. The following year, the teacher invited me back to show the film at the beginning of the semester. He wanted his next class to envision the possibilities as they embarked on their assignment for the semester.

That story demonstrates the power of *Craft*. It's the dominant motivator for approximately a third of today's workforce (including me). And even when it's not dominant, it's a prominent motivator for almost everyone. Whether you're a leader of a global company, or just starting your first job after finishing school, you owe it to yourself to become aware of the role Craft plays in fueling a person's ability to achieve maximum performance.

When we hear the word "craft," our minds often leap to tangible items, carefully wrought by expert hands—a woodworker carving intricate designs into a piece of timber, a potter molding clay on a wheel, or a tailor meticulously stitching fabric into a bespoke suit. These images, while emblematic of craftsmanship, only capture a fraction of its essence. In the broader world of work, and particularly within the confines of the modern workplace, *Craft* signifies something much more profound. It becomes an embodiment of passion, commitment, and the relentless pursuit of mastery.

Craft, as a concept, cannot be constrained to mere manual professions or traditional arts. Instead, it permeates every industry, every role, and every job title. Think of the software developer who spends hours refining a few lines of code, not merely to make it functional but to optimize its elegance and efficiency. Or consider the financial analyst, poring over spreadsheets, refining and re-refining projections to ensure they are as accurate and insightful as possible. These professionals, much like the woodworker or the potter, are driven by a deeper need to be the best at what they do. This innate desire, this compulsion to elevate one's work from mere functionality to an art form, epitomizes Craft.

Why, though, does this matter in today's fast-paced, results-driven workplace environment? After all, isn't the bottom line about productivity, profits, and performance metrics? On the surface, it might appear so. But delve a little deeper, and you'll recognize that businesses thrive not just on quantitative results but on the qualitative contributions of their employees. Employees driven by Craft are not just workers; they are artisans in their domains. Their commitment to their craft means they aren't merely completing tasks; they're refining, innovating, and pushing boundaries, ensuring the output is of the highest possible quality.

But Craft is more than just the end result—it's about the journey. It's about the hours, days, or even years of practice, learning, and growth. It's about the satisfaction that comes from facing a challenging problem and devising an innovative solution. It's about the small victories, like perfecting a method, and the setbacks that offer invaluable lessons. For those driven by Craft, the process is just as valuable, if not more so, than the final product.

In the workplace, this translates to an intrinsic motivation that's vital. Employees who embody the spirit of Craft are self-driven. They seek feedback not just for validation but as a tool to refine their skills further. They are lifelong learners, continuously looking for ways to improve, innovate, and excel. And importantly, they inspire those around them. Their dedication and commitment often act as a beacon, motivating peers and setting a benchmark for excellence.

Moreover, Craft is both personal and collective. On a personal level, Craft is about individual growth, mastery, and fulfillment. On a collective level, it's about performing as a team, with each person playing a vital part. It's about contributing to the organization's success, and driving toward a final outcome. When harnessed, Craft is a motivator that can be seen in the quality of work, the innovative solutions to complex problems, and the drive to constantly do the best work possible. For Craft-dominant workers, it's the main source of satisfaction derived from a job well done and in the admiration of peers and superiors. It's imperative to recognize and value Craft, not just as a skill but as a mindset, a motivation, and a key contributor to both personal and organizational success.

Craft Runs Deep

The essence of human evolution has been marked by our capacity to learn, adapt, and master new skills. From our ancestors mastering the art of fire to modern man's ability to code and build digital worlds, the continuum remains unchanged. This drive for mastery isn't a recent phenomenon birthed by complex job markets or the nuances of the digital age. Instead, it's an intrinsic aspect of our psyche, rooted deeply in our evolutionary history.

Throughout time, the acquisition of skills wasn't just a hobby or a pastime; it was a determinant of survival. Those who could master the art of hunting, foraging, or later, farming, had a competitive edge, ensuring not only their survival but also a certain status within their communities. This drive has transformed over millennia, but the core principle remains: mastery equates to both personal fulfillment and societal value.

In the contemporary workplace, this manifests as a yearning to be proficient, to stand out, and to deliver with excellence. Employees are no longer content with just "doing" a job; they seek to master it. This desire stems not only from external motivations such as promotions or accolades but from a deep-seated need for self-fulfillment and purpose. To master a craft is to know one's role in the larger scheme of things, to find significance in one's contributions.

Recognizing this inherent human trait, modern organizations and leaders can better cater to the needs of their workforce, creating environments that nurture, challenge, and reward the pursuit of mastery.

The Brain Chemistry of Craft

At the very heart of our brain's reward system is dopamine, a neurotransmitter responsible for pleasure, motivation, and learning. When we engage in activities that are challenging yet achievable, and subsequently master them, our brain releases dopamine. This isn't merely an accidental byproduct; it's an evolutionary mechanism. Our ancestors, upon mastering a task critical for survival, experienced this pleasurable dopamine rush, reinforcing the importance of that learned skill.

In the context of Craft, this means every time an individual successfully practices or hones a skill, they're rewarded with a natural high. Whether it's a barista perfecting the art of coffee-making, a writer finding the right words, or a technician troubleshooting a complex problem, the result is the same: a surge of satisfaction, a sense of achievement.

This dopamine-driven feedback loop is incredibly potent. It doesn't just reward the mastery of skills; it drives the desire to continue learning, refining, and perfecting. This intrinsic motivator is a cornerstone of why Craft is such a powerful force in the workplace.

Beyond neurotransmitters and brain chemistry, there's a deeper, more soulful aspect to Craft. Crafting, in its purest form, is a dance between the conscious and the subconscious mind. It is where logic meets creativity, precision meets intuition, and knowledge meets exploration.

Consider the rhythm a potter finds as they shape clay on the wheel. It's not just about the physical act; it's about being in a state of flow, a term popularized by psychologist Mihaly Csikszentmihalyi. Flow is described as that optimal state where a person is so engrossed in an activity that the world around them fades away. Time seems to distort, and there's a profound sense of being 'in the zone.'

The experience of flow is not restricted to artists or craftsmen. An accountant, neck-deep in spreadsheets, or a sales manager inspiring his team well, can experience the same state of heightened focus and immersion. This state brings not just heightened productivity, but also a profound sense of joy and satisfaction. It's a psychological affirmation of one's capability, of being perfectly aligned with a task, and of transcending the mundane.

Craft - An Internal Motivator

For decades, organizational psychology has explored the balance between extrinsic and intrinsic motivators. Extrinsic motivators are external rewards or penalties – think salaries, promotions, or the threat of job loss. While powerful, they have limitations. For one, their motivational effect can diminish over time. Moreover, they can often lead to short-term thinking or even undesirable behaviors if misaligned with organizational goals.

In contrast, intrinsic motivators are internal rewards. The joy derived from mastering a skill, the satisfaction of solving a complex problem, or the thrill of innovation are all intrinsic in nature. They aren't doled out by managers or HR departments, but are self-generated, stemming from the very nature of the task and the individual's relationship with it.

Craft, as a concept, heavily leans on intrinsic motivation. The drive to perfect a skill, to be known for one's mastery, and to continually push boundaries comes from within. It's a motivator that's sustainable, aligned with long-term growth, and immensely fulfilling. Organizations that recognize and nurture this intrinsic drive often find their employees more engaged, innovative, and loyal. They aren't just working for a paycheck; they're working for passion, purpose, and personal growth.

Craft Drives Continuous Improvement

The allure of Craft lies in its perpetual nature. Mastery is not a final destination but a continuous journey. This journey, however, is not always smooth. It's marked by challenges, plateaus, and sometimes even regressions. Yet, it's precisely this balance between challenge and skill that makes Craft so enticing.

If a task is too easy, it becomes mundane and fails to engage. If it's too hard, it can lead to frustration and demotivation. The sweet spot is when the challenge presented is just a notch above the current skill level. It's achievable, but not without effort. This balance keeps the journey of mastery interesting, rewarding, and perpetually engaging.

For organizations, understanding this balance is crucial. It means providing opportunities that stretch employees, allowing them to grow, but without overwhelming them. It's about fostering an environment where challenges are seen as opportunities for growth, and where the journey of mastering a craft is celebrated as much as the mastery itself.

The Return to Craft

In today's digitized, fast-paced world, much of our existence is marked by fleeting interactions, ephemeral trends, and rapid consumption. The rise of automation and instant gratification has brought undeniable benefits, but also an unforeseen side effect: a collective yearning for the genuine, the lasting, and the masterful. The resurgence of artisanal movements—from hand-crafted goods to specialty foods—reflects society's desire for authenticity and a connection to the 'real.'

Craft, in this context, becomes more than just skill mastery; it's a statement against disposability, a nod towards the timeless, and a pursuit of meaning in an age of abundance but often lacking depth.

With the diminishment of traditional societal roles and the rise of individualism, identity formation has shifted. Increasingly, people are looking to their professions, passions, and skills as central pillars of their identity. The mastery of a craft is no longer just about the skill itself, but about how that skill allows for self-expression, distinction, and personal narrative.

For many, being recognized for one's craft is an affirmation of their unique place in the world. In a society where so much is mass-produced, the craftsman stands out, not just for their expertise, but for their dedication to a path less traveled—a path of continuous learning, refinement, and authenticity.

Cultivating Craft in the Workplace

Modern organizations have a unique role and responsibility in this cultural resurgence of Craft. The workplace isn't just a space for task completion; it's a space for self-actualization. Organizations that recognize and foster an environment conducive to mastery stand to benefit immensely. Such environments not only enhance skill sets but also allow employees to intertwine their professional and personal identities.

By creating opportunities for learning, by celebrating milestones of mastery, and by valuing the uniqueness of each employee's craft, organizations can cultivate a sense of belonging and purpose. When employees see their workplace as a canvas for their craft, their commitment to the organization deepens, and their output resonates with genuine passion and excellence.

From the rising popularity of documentaries showcasing craftsmen to the global fascination with hand-made, bespoke products, popular culture is rife with examples of Craft's allure. Consider the boom in craft beer, where every brewer infuses their unique touch, story, and technique into each bottle. Or the resurgence of vinyl records in an age of digital streaming, signaling a longing for tactile, authentic experiences.

These trends aren't just nostalgic; they highlight society's need to balance the modern with the meaningful. They underscore the value of patience, dedication, and mastery in a world of instant results.

Everyday Craft

While not every job role can mimic the traditional craftsman's tangible outputs, the underlying principles of Craft can be translated to even the most modern professions. A software developer, for instance, can approach coding with the same dedication and finesse as a carpenter sculpting wood. An HR professional can curate organizational culture with the meticulousness of a painter crafting a masterpiece.

The key lies in shifting perceptions. Instead of viewing tasks as mere checkboxes, employees can be encouraged to see them as opportunities for mastery, for adding a unique touch, and for continuous refinement. Leaders and managers play a crucial role here, by setting expectations not just for completion but for craftsmanship.

While the merits of Craft are many, fostering a workplace culture centered around it isn't without challenges. Not all tasks lend themselves easily to mastery, and not all employees might resonate with the craftsman mindset. There's a fine line between encouraging mastery and inadvertently promoting perfectionism, which can lead to burnout.

Moreover, in industries driven by rapid outputs and tight timelines, the slow, deliberate nature of Craft might seem at odds with organizational objectives. Leaders looking to imbue a sense of Craft in their teams must find the balance between efficiency and mastery, between speed and depth.

The modern resurgence of Craft, both in society and the workplace, is a testament to the timeless human need for meaning, mastery, and authentic self-expression. As the lines between personal and professional identities blur, and as the world grapples with the dichotomies of modernity, Craft emerges as a beacon, illuminating a path towards genuine fulfillment and excellence.

Recruiting for Craft

When seeking potential employees, it's essential to look beyond mere qualifications and experience. Talent acquisition strategies that recognize and prioritize craft-oriented candidates can bring in individuals with a deeper commitment to their roles. Such individuals often exhibit traits like passion, dedication, and an insatiable hunger to refine their skills. By developing interview questions and assessments that gauge an individual's relationship with their craft, organizations can filter in candidates that align with this philosophy.

Craft is not just about possessing a skill but about the relentless pursuit of refining it. Organizations must reevaluate their training and development programs to ensure they are not just about imparting knowledge but about fostering mastery. This means providing resources, tools, and opportunities that allow employees to delve deep, practice, and perfect. Whether it's sponsoring advanced courses, facilitating workshops, or creating platforms for peer-to-peer learning, the goal should be to cultivate a craftsman's mindset.

The journey towards mastering a craft is as much about doing as it is about reflecting. Organizations should create spaces—both physical and metaphorical—where employees can practice, make mistakes, learn, and reflect on their journey. This could mean setting up dedicated innovation labs, promoting 'side projects', or simply encouraging teams to allocate time for deep work without the pressures of deadlines or deliverables.

Recognizing and Celebrating Craft

For the craftsman, validation of their mastery is crucial. Organizations must build mechanisms to recognize and celebrate moments of mastery. This doesn't always mean grand awards or bonuses. Sometimes, a genuine acknowledgment from a leader, a showcase of the employee's work, or an opportunity to share their craft with peers can be deeply rewarding. By creating a culture that regularly celebrates craft, organizations can foster motivation and a sense of pride among their teams.

One of the unique aspects of modern organizations is the diversity of skills and crafts under one roof. By creating platforms where different craftsmen can collaborate, share, and learn from each other, organizations can spark innovation. An engineer can learn nuances from a designer, a writer can gain insights from a data analyst, and so forth. Such cross-pollination can lead to novel solutions, products, and services while also enriching each individual's craft.

While the concept of Craft is timeless, its application in the ever-evolving organizational landscape requires periodic reassessment. Leaders should regularly revisit their strategies, gather feedback, and make necessary adjustments to ensure the culture of Craft remains vibrant and relevant.

Significance, Identity, and Craft

At its core, identity answers the profound question: Who am I? In modern times, where the boundaries between personal and professional selves blur, the workplace has become a significant space for identity exploration and affirmation. Gone are the days when work was merely a means to an end; for many, their professional roles are intertwined with their self-concept and self-worth.

Craft goes beyond the mere act of doing. It's a celebration of the individual's unique approach, creativity, and perspective. As craftsmen hone their skills, they're also weaving their narratives, stories, and personal touches into their work. Every brush stroke, every code line, every handcrafted piece becomes a testament to their individuality. Through craft, workers aren't just producing; they're expressing.

The journey to mastering a craft is rife with challenges, introspection, and growth. Every milestone achieved, every challenge overcome adds another layer to the craftsman's identity. This journey strengthens their connection with their profession, making it an integral part of who they are. It's no longer just about what they do, but how they do it and why they do it.

There's an unparalleled sense of fulfillment in being recognized for one's craft. When peers, leaders, or clients acknowledge and appreciate the mastery, it solidifies the craftsman's place in the professional community. This recognition isn't just about external validation; it's an affirmation of the craftsman's choices, efforts, and dedication. Being known for one's craft becomes a powerful part of their identity, a badge of honor that distinguishes them in a sea of professionals.

When workers express and solidify their identities through their crafts, it creates a ripple effect in the workplace. A culture that values craftsmanship breeds mutual respect, admiration, and collaboration. Workers no longer see each other as mere colleagues but as artisans with unique stories, insights, and contributions. Such an environment fosters deeper connections, collaborations, and a collective pursuit of excellence.

Practical Steps for Organizations

Every workforce has a segment of individuals inherently driven by the motivation of Craft. These individuals are naturally wired to find deep satisfaction in mastery and the art of their work. It's crucial for talent acquisition and HR teams to identify such candidates during the recruitment process. Beyond recognizing them, it's equally vital to ensure they are placed in roles where their inherent drive for craftsmanship can shine and be nurtured. Pairing them with like-minded mentors can further amplify their potential and satisfaction.

Given the unique intrinsic motivation of the Craft-driven subset of employees, generic growth opportunities might not always suffice. Specialized workshops, advanced courses tailored to deep skill refinement, and dedicated time slots for experimentation can be invaluable for this group. By recognizing their inherent need to challenge and refine their skills, organizations can create a roadmap that ensures these craftsmen continually evolve within the company's ecosystem.

While the Craft-driven workforce is a particular segment, integrating Craft values into the company's culture can benefit the entire organization.

By doing so, businesses not only cater to the natural inclinations of the Craft-driven individuals but also inspire others to explore and find joy in mastery. Regular celebrations of craftsmanship milestones, both big and small, can motivate and instill a sense of pride. Cross-functional collaborations can also enable Craft-driven employees to merge their expertise with others, leading to innovative outcomes.

Craft or Crumble

The nature of work is in constant flux. Technological advancements, globalization, and a newfound emphasis on work-life harmony have all played pivotal roles in reshaping how we perceive our professional lives. Yet, amidst this whirlwind of change, one ancient principle has regained prominence: the intrinsic value of Craft.

Craft, in its essence, is the passionate pursuit of mastery. It's not about merely performing a task but immersing oneself in it, understanding its intricacies, and continuously striving for perfection. Historically, craftsmen were revered in societies – be it the blacksmith whose swords were unparalleled in sharpness or the weaver whose fabric told stories of generations. Their identity was interwoven with their skill, and their craft was a direct reflection of their soul.

Fast forward to today, when automation and artificial intelligence are rapidly taking over repetitive tasks, and the nature of human work is undergoing a seismic shift. It is in this landscape that the significance of Craft stands out even more starkly. As machines handle the mundane, humans have the opportunity, and perhaps the responsibility, to delve deeper into roles that require creativity, empathy, innovation, and yes, craftsmanship.

The contemporary workplace, characterized by digital nomadism, remote work, and a mosaic of diverse roles, offers a fertile ground for Craft to flourish. As tasks become more specialized and niche, there is a burgeoning space for individuals to become masters in their chosen fields. Graphic designers, software developers, content creators, and even data scientists, to name a few, have the potential to elevate their work from mere tasks to an art form, a craft. Every line of code can be poetic, every design can narrate a tale, and every analysis can uncover a universe of insights.

Moreover, the evolving work ethos, characterized by a search for meaning and purpose, aligns seamlessly with the principles of Craft. Millennials and Gen Z, who now form a significant chunk of the workforce, aren't just looking for jobs; they're in pursuit of vocations that resonate with their identity. For them, work isn't just about monetary compensation. It's about passion, growth, and the satisfaction derived from excelling in their chosen domain. This mindset creates a natural inclination towards Craft, as these generations seek to embed their essence into their work.

Organizations, too, are recognizing the potential of fostering a culture of Craft. In an age where brand differentiation is often minimal, it's craftsmanship that can set a product or service apart. It's the human touch, the attention to detail, the finesse of a master that can elevate an ordinary product to extraordinary. As such, businesses that prioritize and nurture Craft not only boost employee satisfaction and retention but also carve a unique space for themselves in the market.

However, this renewed emphasis on Craft is not without challenges in the modern workplace. Balancing the pursuit of perfection inherent in craftsmanship with the rapid pace of today's business world can be daunting. Moreover, as workplaces become more diverse and dispersed, ensuring that the essence of Craft isn't lost in translation requires conscious effort.

In conclusion, as the workplace landscape continues to evolve, it's evident that the ancient ethos of Craft has found its rightful place in the modern era. It serves as a bridge between the past and the future, reminding us that while tools and technologies might change, the human spirit's drive for mastery remains unwavering. The future of work, it seems, will be a harmonious blend of innovation and craftsmanship, with Craft leading the way in adding soul to the machine.

Steps to Consider when Craft Scores are Low

When a Culture MRI® analysis shows low Craft scores, it means that the company fails to feed an important motivation. For many employees, work is an outlet for contributing a unique skill. It's satisfying to possess a valuable ability and to offer it to the company's process. Ironically, this is precisely what the company needs. However, it can be overlooked. The main reason this gap occurs is that leaders have a different dominant motivation such as Cause or Community. When this happens, leaders typically resort to emphasizing their own motivator. They emphasize the Cause or foster Community instead of celebrating the excellent skills of the Craft-motivated employee. The solution is rather simple. Regardless of the leaders' own biases, companies should install practices that regularly emphasize the role of Craft in the organization. Consider these steps of correction:

- Create recognition programs for Craft
- Showcase the role of Craft in internal communications
- Emphasize Craft in the training experience
- Make sure Craft is reflected in the core values
- Measure, celebrate, and reward Craft in performance management

For additional resources, please visit www.theculturemri.com.

Reflect:
How motivating is craft for you?

CHAPTER 18

C2: CAUSE

Ernest Shackleton was an explorer of Antarctica in the early 1900s. The story goes that he used reverse psychology to recruit crewmen for one treacherous journey. The ad he placed in the newspaper promised, "...low wages, bitter cold, and long hours of complete darkness...." Shackleton's office was overrun with eager applicants. The ad itself has never actually been sourced, and attempts to research the story's origins seem to write it off as a myth. Regardless, the tale manages to illustrate the power of Cause to motivate workers.

When something really matters to you, there's almost nothing you won't do to pursue it, build it, nurture it, or protect it. That's what a Cause represents. It can be an ideal, an accomplishment, a vision, or a goal. But Cause becomes a motivator when it's something that makes you willing to endure hardship and overcome obstacles to achieve it.

Cause Shapes Identity

As a college freshman, I still had the body of a high school kid. Awkwardly tall, I couldn't put on weight no matter how much or how often I stuffed myself. It seemed like all the other males on campus had facial hair and muscles that could stretch a tank top to its breaking point. I was desperate to find some expression of acceptable manhood.

Toward the end of the school year, to my utter surprise, the head basketball coach approached me after a gym class and said, "I sure wish I could talk you into playing for us." To that point, I'd only played pick-up ball. I wasn't the worst person you've ever seen, but I certainly didn't consider myself college material. I hadn't even played in high school. Somehow, the coach's unlikely invitation made me forget all that. I mean, I was taller than Michael Jordan, and he turned out pretty good. And the coach suggested that he could show me everything I needed to do. All I had to do was show up and work hard.

As I began to imagine myself suiting up with the real men of the college basketball team, a new hope was growing inside me. I didn't know how to become a college athlete. I had no idea. But here was a paid professional offering to take me through a process that might just solve my manhood troubles. Being labeled as an athlete would somehow make up for being a bit of a late bloomer. It was like the coach was offering me a side door into masculinity. I was all in.

From that moment, I was motivated by a Cause that would consume me: to make the team the next year. My strategy was simple. Do everything the coach told me to do, and do it with all my being.

For the next nine months, my life revolved around basketball. I worked out, ran drills, scrimmaged, and conditioned. Some of it was a blast. And some of it was the worst physical suffering I'd ever experienced. But I didn't care. I was ready to endure anything for the sake of the Cause that would redefine my identity.

The next fall, I made the team, although I'm sure it was based on my developmental potential and not my fledgling skills. I played the whole season and saw action in some of the unimportant games. Despite my progress, I realized I'd never catch up enough to make a meaningful contribution to the team. So I dropped basketball after one year.

But I'll never forget the lesson it taught me: Cause is a powerful motivator!

Of all the workplace motivations, Cause (or Purpose) may be the most commonly referenced and least understood. Rooted in the innate human desire for purpose, Cause refers to the profound urge to contribute to something deemed essential or meaningful. In the dynamic fabric of modern workplaces, tapping into this motivator can result in not just productivity but a deeper sense of fulfillment and satisfaction. This chapter explores the impact, breadth, and depth of Cause within workplace culture.

Throughout history, humans have consistently yearned for purpose and meaning. This universal aspiration isn't just a philosophical pondering or a cultural construct; it's deeply rooted in our psychology and brain chemistry. Understanding the psychology behind the Cause gives us a deeper appreciation for its powerful and transformative nature in both personal and professional arenas.

The Two Manifestations of Cause

Cause can be manifested in one of two forms: *relevant* or *transcendent*. The two can look quite different from each other, even though they impact engagement and culture with equal power. So I should take a moment to define each of these unique manifestations.

A relevant cause is a purpose whose rewards come in the form of recognition and attention. That's what drove my commitment to basketball — achieving the goal of becoming an athlete was extremely relevant to me. The success of the school's basketball program (not to mention my own) was a cause that had a direct impact on me personally.

In the workplace, examples of people driven by the *relevant* form of cause are all around us.

For example, some Starbucks baristas get their primary satisfaction from being at the center of an iconic brand. All day long, customers line up to get a beverage that is symbolic of their day. Entrepreneurs, business pioneers, home-makers, and sales reps gather each morning in line. In effect, Starbucks plays a key role in fueling these diverse economic engines. The barista can't help feeling like the catalyst for the whole thing. The job feels relevant to current events.

A *transcendent* cause has subtle differences from its counterpart, *relevant* cause. Its power doesn't require that the bearer has something relevant to gain or lose personally from the arrangement, thus lighting a fire under the feet. Instead, those who are inspired by transcendent cause are effectively motivated by the pure ideals themselves that hang in the balance of doing the work. This type is altruism, plain and simple.

A transcendent cause is a purpose whose value is found in one or more core values and is commonly referred to as a "higher calling." Serving in the Peace Corps, working in ministry, curing a deadly disease, and reversing pollution are a few examples. These transcendent causes produce an inner sense of "rightness" about the work. This type of worker is often driven by a burning desire to right a wrong, to relieve a pain, or to correct an injustice in the world. The transcendent manifestation requires less recognition and attention than the relevant one. An inner satisfaction is felt just from knowing the situation is addressed, whether others happen to notice or not.

The Brain Chemistry of Cause

When we talk about Cause in terms of human motivation, we're referring to the intrinsic desire to contribute to something bigger than oneself. In the case of relevant cause, it's a bigger community; in the case of transcendent cause, it's a bigger mission. This desire is not arbitrary; it's intertwined with the very architecture of our brains. But how does a purpose or Cause influence our brain's chemistry?

One of the most critical neurotransmitters to consider here is serotonin. Known popularly as the "feel-good" chemical, serotonin plays an intricate role in mood regulation, feelings of well-being, and happiness. Beyond these functions, serotonin is also intimately associated with social behavior and feelings of significance or importance.

When individuals connect with a Cause or a purpose, their brain perceives this alignment as a positive and meaningful social interaction. This is because being part of a bigger purpose or contributing to a collective cause is inherently a social endeavor. When we feel we matter in this grand scheme, our brain rewards us by releasing serotonin. This not only elevates our mood but also fortifies our connection to that particular Cause, creating a virtuous cycle. The more we engage with the Cause, the better we feel, urging us to delve deeper and contribute more.

This serotonin release also explains why individuals who identify with a Cause often exhibit higher resilience, especially in challenging situations. A robust sense of purpose can act as an emotional buffer, and the associated serotonin release can counteract feelings of stress or anxiety, ensuring that individuals remain committed and motivated even when the going gets tough.

Moreover, from an evolutionary perspective, our ancestors thrived on community and cooperation. Those who worked towards a collective Cause or purpose, like hunting or gathering as a group, had higher survival rates. As a result, our brains have evolved to reward these cooperative behaviors. The brain recognizes actions that contribute to a larger purpose as beneficial for both the individual and the community and, in turn, releases serotonin as a positive reinforcement mechanism.

But the effects of Cause on our psychology aren't limited to serotonin alone. Other neurotransmitters and hormones, like dopamine (associated with reward and pleasure) and oxytocin (linked to social bonding and trust), also come into play. When we align with a Cause, the feeling of accomplishment and the bonds we form with others on the same journey lead to a release of these chemicals, further enhancing our commitment and satisfaction.

The human inclination towards Cause and purpose is not merely a lofty ideal. It is a concrete, biochemically-driven phenomenon that has profound implications for our well-being, resilience, and overall happiness. The interplay between Cause and brain chemistry, particularly serotonin, underscores the importance of finding and connecting with purpose, be it in personal pursuits or within the workplace. Not only does it elevate our mood and motivation, but it also solidifies our position as social beings, eager to contribute and make a difference in the world around us.

Historically, humans have always sought meaning in their actions. From ancient civilizations building monuments to honor their gods to revolutionaries fighting for causes they believed in, there's an ingrained need to be part of something bigger. In the workplace, this translates to Cause as a primary source of job satisfaction.

Feeling impactful is not just a "nice-to-have"; it's a psychological necessity. Maslow's hierarchy places self-actualization at its pinnacle – and finding purpose in one's work is a direct route to achieving that. When employees resonate with the Cause they're contributing to, it serves as an intrinsic motivation, often more potent than extrinsic rewards.

The "Cause Person" Defined

Who exactly is a Cause person? Imagine an individual who doesn't just work for a paycheck or promotion but dives deep into projects because they genuinely believe in the ripple effects of their efforts. It's the Peace Corps volunteer enduring hardships to make a community self-reliant or the minister dedicating their life to spiritual guidance.

But Cause isn't confined to altruistic domains. Consider a software developer at a start-up, fervently coding because they believe their app will revolutionize how society functions. The key? Feeling like a cog in the wheel of change.

At a bustling Apple Genius Bar, a technician troubleshoots a device. To an outsider, it may appear mundane. But for the technician, they're on the frontlines of a technological revolution, contributing to global digital evolution. This highlights Cause's range: from intimate personal purposes to being part of global movements.

Cause can vary in scale but remains universal in impact. Whether it's the satisfaction of supporting local community growth or being a tiny dot in a vast, global initiative, the underpinning desire remains consistent: making a difference.

The Benefits of Cause

Companies that leverage Cause as a motivation enjoy a unique set of advantages:

1. Increased Engagement: Employees are not just physically present; they're mentally and emotionally invested.
2. Enhanced Satisfaction: A job isn't just a series of tasks; it's a mission that brings fulfillment.
3. Organizational Gains: Reduced attrition rates and enhanced loyalty lead to sustainable growth.

Steps to Consider when Cause Scores are Low

Cause is not a modern-day fad; it's a timeless human need. As workplaces continue to evolve, recognizing and harnessing the power of Cause will be crucial. Not just for business growth, but for creating workplaces where individuals feel valued, impactful, and truly alive. The rise of technology and globalization amplifies cause-driven motivations, with younger generations particularly prioritizing purpose over paychecks. The future will likely see a surge in organizations that embed Cause at their core, viewing it not as an option but a necessity.

When a Culture MRI® analysis shows low Cause scores, there could be a variety of underlying reasons. Essentially, employees see no purpose for the work they do every day, either because it's not obvious, or because it's not celebrated adequately. It's up to the leaders to make sure this connection is evident and relevant. Furthermore, leaders must observe certain principles when doing so.

Most importantly, the Cause must be something that benefits the employee. For example, the cause of growing the company may not be a perceived benefit to the average person. Sure, it benefits the owners, but who's to say that makes life better for anyone else? Skepticism might arise if employees feel the Cause is just a corporate façade. Additionally, personal and company causes might sometimes diverge.

Overcoming these challenges requires authentic leadership, regular communication, and fostering a culture of openness. Leaders should be prepared to evolve the company's Cause in line with changing times and societal needs, ensuring it remains relevant and resonant. By creating an environment that resonates with Cause, businesses can optimize their most valuable asset: human capital. But it can't be a mere buzzword; it must be deeply integrated into the culture. To accomplish this, leaders can:

Articulate the Cause: Make the organization's purpose clear and communicable.
Integrate into Vision: Let the cause be the compass guiding the company's strategic decisions.
Provide Opportunities: Allow employees to see their direct impact, be it through feedback loops, open dialogues, or impact reports.

Consider these steps of correction:

- Create recognition programs for Cause
- Showcase the Cause in internal communications
- Emphasize Cause in the training experience
- Make sure Cause is reflected in the core values
- Measure, celebrate, and reward Cause in performance management

For additional resources, please visit www.theculturemri.com.

Reflect:
How motivating is cause for you?

CHAPTER 19

C3: COMMUNITY

They paint their faces, neck, and upper body with multi-colored grease paint. They adorn their carriages with ribbons and streamers and flags. They arrive a half-day before kickoff, offering up choice meats on altars of iron and steel. Music blares as gathering tribes chant ceremonial calls to demonstrate their allegiance. It's football Saturday. And for millions of Americans, this is what life is all about.

For the moment, let's overlook the tenuous connections by which these frenzied followers base their citizenship in this fan nation. Apparently, all are welcome.

At the University of Michigan, "The Big House" as it's called is built to accommodate 107,601 onlookers for home games. This makes the stadium the seventh-largest city in the state on game day. But Michigan is just the tip of this colossal iceberg. Nearly a dozen stadiums in the country match the capacity of The Big House. Memorial Stadium, home of the Cornhuskers, becomes the third-largest city in Nebraska during home games. Collectively, more than 47 million people gather for games during any single season, which equates to roughly one person out of every seven American citizens.

NFL teams boast an even bigger following. The largest belongs to the Dallas Cowboys, with nearly 10 million fans with a history of more than 200 consecutive sold-out games. The franchise is valued at over $4 billion.

Of the 90 players who make up the Dallas Cowboy's roster, only eight were actually born in the Dallas metro area. The overwhelming majority hail from places with allegiances to competitors of the Cowboys. That's the business side of the game. Players are drafted, signed, and traded like commodities then suited up in the team's colors for game day. Many trades happen mid-season, essentially swapping players with rival teams. Each year, coaches and players pass through the revolving doors that separate one franchise from the next. The average NFL career only lasts 3.3 years. Some veterans have played for three or four different teams during their careers. Meanwhile, teams update uniforms, introduce new mascots, and build new stadiums. Over time, everything but the name of the team changes. That's the business of football – But fans don't seem to mind. Football is a business run by a small handful of owners and managers. Essentially, football fans spend their time and money to watch other people do their jobs. Have you ever considered selling tickets to let people watch you work? Can you imagine the cheers as you hit send on an email, close a sale, or clock out after an epic week?

The typical fan is often a transplant as well, sometimes dividing loyalties between two or more teams. 71% of NFL fans claim to be supporters of more than one team.

During Super Bowl week, 72% of Americans identify as football fans. Of the 113 million viewers of the game, fewer than 10% can actually claim membership in the fanbase of either of the two remaining teams. The rest tag along as secondary fans or curious bystanders. What they all share in common is a general desire to participate.

America is a nation of fans. But this phenomenon is not unique to the U.S. Globally, the sports industry generates nearly half a trillion dollars each year. The FIFA Women's World Cup, for example, reaches an audience of approximately 2 billion fans. International soccer fans show their dedication by chanting and swaying in an almost trance-like state for the entire 90-minutes of their matches. Needless to say, they come decked out in team jerseys and all related paraphernalia to show their tribal alliances.

For a segment of those touched by fandom, the commitment approaches intoxication. According to one study, when France hosted and won the World Cup in 1998, the suicide rate dropped by more than 10%. Conversely, fans seeking to express disappointment often besiege their own towns. When the Philadelphia Eagles lost to the Kansas City Chiefs on a last-second field goal, fans rioted, setting fires and smashing windows on the way to racking up millions of dollars in damages across metro Philadelphia.

The need to belong is a powerful human driver. According to Dr. Daniel Wann, professor of psychology at Murray State University, fans identify with sports teams the same way people identify with a nationality or ethnicity. In other words, fandom fills a need traditionally met by geopolitical or tribal affiliations. Wann research points to several core needs behind our interest in sports. One is the need to belong. When someone roots for a team, they are transformed from a "me" to a "we." That's empowering.

In contrast, teams sometimes offer fans an opportunity to distinguish themselves from the mainstream. Some have called this impulse "peacocking," a reference to putting forward an ornate display in order to broadcast one's unique worth. Following an unusual or offbeat team like Ball State or Dartmouth creates intrigue and reminds us that wins and losses aren't the only determiner of value for a sub-culture. Atlanta's Oglethorpe University hasn't had a football team since 1941, when all men's sports were shut down by World War II. Nevertheless, die-hard fans still express their pride by wearing sweatshirts that say, "Oglethorpe Football - Undefeated since 1941."

As I've emphasized throughout this book, understanding what drives employees is paramount for organizational success. We've looked at several motivations so far. In this chapter, we'll look at a core motivation called "Community." This motivation shapes our work lives, influences brain chemistry, and impacts our overall well-being.

Defining Community in a Workplace Setting

Community, in the context of the workplace, goes beyond merely working together. It signifies a deeper connection, a feeling of belonging, and a sense of mutual support. It is when individuals no longer see themselves as mere employees but as essential parts of a collective. This cohesive bond impacts motivation, productivity, and job satisfaction. Beyond the subjective feeling of belonging, the human brain provides tangible evidence of the power of community.

Enter oxytocin, often termed the 'love' or 'bonding' hormone. This neurotransmitter plays a crucial role in human connection, bonding, and social interactions. When individuals feel connected or experience a sense of belonging, there is a surge in oxytocin levels. This not only promotes bonding but also has several beneficial effects like reducing anxiety, fostering trust, and encouraging collaboration. In a workplace setting, when employees feel they're part of a community, their brains release oxytocin, making them more trustful of colleagues, more engaged, and generally happier. This hormone can prove extremely valuable to a company's bottom line.

Community, Engagement, and Well-being

For community-driven employees, three core needs stand out. First is the sense of belonging. This isn't about merely fitting in but feeling valued and understood. Second, community implies an element of irreplaceability – the notion that the employee plays a unique, non-substitutable role in the team. Third, community suggests social support – interactions that go beyond work, fostering deeper connections and mutual support. When this trifecta is present, it constitutes a strong sense of community in the workplace that directly correlates with job satisfaction. Employees who feel they belong are more likely to be engaged, motivated, and loyal.

These employees are also likely to experience higher productivity, reduced turnover, and enhanced collaboration. A sense of community breaks down silos, encouraging cross-departmental interaction and teamwork. Various studies back these claims. For instance, a Gallup survey found that employees with strong workplace connections boast a 7% higher productivity rate.

Identifying The Community Motivation

Consider two technicians at the Apple Store Genius Bar. Technician A loves his job because he's an expert at any craft involving Apple products. Technician B, however, is motivated by something completely different: community. Although both technicians seem equally enthusiastic, it's actually for two different reasons. Technician B enjoys his role primarily because of the connections with colleagues. At first glance one might assume that both are motivated for the same reason. That misunderstanding could prove disruptive and costly. It's crucial to distinguish technician B's primary driver – a sense of community – from the other. For technician B, whether it's front-of-house customer interactions or backroom inventory sorting, as long as he feels connected, he's content. This highlights the nuanced differences between the motivations of the self-actualized worker.

Fulfilling the Need for Community

Neglecting community needs in the workplace can lead to consequences. Without a sense of belonging, employees can feel alienated, leading to decreased engagement. At the very least, they are more likely to seek community outside the workplace. Having a life beyond work is certainly reasonable; however, the more employees are driven to other sources to meet the need for community, the more it dilutes from bonds they could be developing at work. To reiterate, the goal is not to build one-dimensional cultish teams; but fostering community represents a huge opportunity to make the organization a prime source of a core, human need. When executed successfully, it eliminates the need to look for outside sources that invariably distract from or possibly conflict with their professional roles. Addressing this need proactively within the organization is, therefore, not just beneficial but essential.

Steps to Consider when Community Scores are Low

Community isn't a mere buzzword; it's a powerful motivator that can shape workplace experiences. In the modern workplace, it's not just about individual achievements but the collective success and bond that truly drive performance and satisfaction.

When a Culture MRI® reveals suppressed Community scores, there are several strategies for fostering a stronger sense of community. Here are several:

- Promote teamwork by encouraging projects that require collaboration
- Introduce social interactions such as team outings, lunches, or simple coffee breaks
- Use recognition to highlight and value each employee's unique contribution
- Create channels where employees can share ideas, concerns, and even personal stories
- Set the tone by promoting inclusivity; avoid creating cliques that can alienate others
- Provide resources and training to nurture community-centric values within teams
- Avoid mandatory fun. It can lead to resentment rather than genuine bonding
- While community is essential, it shouldn't overshadow individual talents or other motivations
- Ensure efforts to build community don't inadvertently exclude certain groups.

For additional resources, please visit www.theculturemri.com.

Reflect:
How motivating is community for you?

THE ARCHITECTS OF CULTURE

*"We can change the world and make it a better place.
It is in our hands to make a difference"*

~ Nelson Mandela

Let's put it all together.

Think of yourself as an architect. Your job, in this case, is to design the culture of an organization. As you sit down at the drafting table, let's review the basics.

Allow yourself to feel the weight of this assignment. A lot is riding on the culture you'll build.

First, there are financial implications. You want to maximize the company's investment in salaries, benefits, training, employee experience… along with all the other efforts the organization makes to attract and retain an effective workforce. This is your chance to create maximum ROI.

Second, the value of your brand is on the line. Part of brand value comes from customer perception. But in today's digitally-connected world, employee perceptions impact the brand too. There's a brand inside the company that makes up half of what the company is worth.

With that in mind, you review the formula for culture:

$C = MVV \times L / Eng$

Culture equals your Mission, Vision and Values… multiplied across your Labor Force… then divided by the level of engagement of your people.

For the sake of this exercise, we'll assume your mission, vision, and values have been determined already. As the architect, you'll be focused on building the level of engagement so employees can align with your MVV.

Your starting point is to measure the status of ALL the factors that influence and determine worker engagement. Remember, this is like aviation. It's not enough just to focus on one or two important factors. You must identify ALL the factors and be able to give a report on their status. Overlook something and the whole organization suffers.

With a thorough evaluation of each of the engagement psychometrics, you conclude that your people are more engaged than the national average. Congratulations! Your overall engagement score of 65% means labor efficiency is pretty good.

Next, you explore the financial effect of engagement. After spending a total of $XX on labor annually (fill in your actual numbers here), you're able to calculate the total losses due to less-than-perfect engagement.

By using a third-party company to conduct the research, your employees are more confident opening up about issues without fear of reprisals. As a result, some previously hidden feedback is now evident. As you examine each individual psychometric, you spot the primary culprit.

In the real-life examples we see at The Culture MRI®, this could be an operational breakdown that makes people frustrated or confused. It might be out-dated training that sets employees up for failure. Or a minor communication breakdown that hampers a crucial hand-off. Sometimes it's a lack of advancement opportunities that leaves people feeling a little like they're stuck in a dead end job. Or it could be the presence of a leadership style that lacks empathy and comes across as "old-school." Any of these issues can contribute to a sense of dissatisfaction that hinders engagement and performance.

In short order, you spot an opportunity. For example, you filter through the data and discover a workload issue that's costing nearly $1M. Upon closer inspection, you determine that understaffing at the regional level has led to a span-of-control shortfall. In other words, it's time to spread the workload more evenly. For a mere $75,000 you can augment the staff to relieve the bottleneck and easily recover half of the leaking $1M. So, for an investment of $75,000, your net improvement is $425,000. And that's just one issue!

Methodically, you work your way through each psychometric. In addition to the raw engagement scores, you dig deeper to understand the user stories that correspond to each one. You collaborate with the leadership team to draft a long-term strategy for optimizing the culture this way during the course of the year.

After one year, you remeasure to analyze progress. By taking the approach of an architect of culture, you've not only recovered millions in lost performance, but employees are happier and work is more enjoyable. Best of all, the CFO can see the precise ROI of these efforts: the company invested a total of $3.1M on improvements, and the data shows a bump in overall profitability of more than $26M!

That's the result of quantifying culture. Human performance is no longer a mystery. Each psychometric is mapped to a specific dollar-value... as well as the remediation steps used to resolve problems and close gaps.

It brings to mind an analogy. Imagine it's a typical afternoon and you're enjoying a nice walk back to the office after lunch. Suddenly, you notice a slight headache developing. You've had this kind of headache before. It's not crippling, but it's unpleasant nonetheless. Up ahead you see the corner drug store. For $5, you can buy a pill that eliminates the headache. You think to yourself, "Is it worth $5 to feel better?" Absolutely it is! An hour later, you're operating at peak performance and feeling great doing it. The $5 you spent is yielding a massive ROI in terms of the quality of your afternoon output.

That's a picture of what it looks like to architect culture.

Research abounds. And all of it points to the fact that the workforce today is operating at a fraction of its potential. Work itself has a headache. We created The Culture MRI® to pinpoint the cause – and the cost – of the headaches that cost companies performance and profitability. In the future, all human resources will be evaluated with similar metrics.

Reflect:
Do you normally think of culture as having tangible value?

EPILOGUE

A MESSAGE FOR THE C-SUITE

"To win in the marketplace you must first win in the workplace."

~ Doug Conant

Culture is money.

It's a form of currency. But if you've never thought of it that way, there's a good reason. Currency is a meaningless concept unless it's accompanied by an accurate system of accounting. That's why previous conversations about culture have probably seemed trivial when compared to things like COGS and EBITDA. There was no method of accounting for culture. And without one, you're left with a mix of seemingly beneficial ideas but no concrete evidence of ROI.

But be careful to pay close attention this time. Once culture is codified, it becomes a manageable discipline. And this one promises to release massive reserves of revenue and profitability for virtually every organization.

Plain and simple, your people are a factor in every equation that matters to the business. Wherever people interact, they take on a distinct culture. And that culture, in turn, impacts market share, profitability, and valuation. It regulates the sense of urgency, the speed of execution, and resiliency to accommodate change for the entire organization.

In some companies culture is a multiplier that translates into market dominance, giant margins, and attractive multiples for the company's valuation. In others, culture is a divisor that hacks into every system in the value chain and silently drains its vigor.

That part is nothing new.

What's different about this moment in time is that the quantification of culture makes it now the single greatest opportunity for most companies. There's untapped potential in the workforce that doesn't exist in product design or process improvement. Those disciplines have been squeezed for every ounce of value.

Human resources, however, are the crude oil just waiting to be refined into fuel. They've been there all along. But the field lacked the sophistication required of business conversations. The technology of refining this raw fuel hadn't been developed.

But now it has.

Culture is no longer just an empty buzz phrase. We now possess the systems and methods of converting raw human potential into specific cultural values that support the business. They've been tested and validated for over ten years with actual companies. Our Culture MRI® algorithms have been the subject of doctoral studies at major universities. A field once comprised of cheap theatrics like casual Fridays and balloon animals is now a legitimate science just waiting to be leveraged by investors.

The Next Industrial Revolution

Since the Industrial Revolution, there have been several mini-revolutions or significant shifts that have reenergized and transformed the general economy.

For example, the Technological Revolution of the late 19th and early 20th Century brought major technological advancements, such as the development of electricity, telegraph, telephone, and internal combustion engines. These innovations drastically changed industries and daily life, leading to increased productivity and new business models.

In the late 20th Century, the so-called Digital Revolution (often associated with the third Industrial Revolution) marked the shift from mechanical and analogue electronic technology to digital electronics. The invention of the personal computer and the internet fundamentally transformed the way businesses operate and how people communicate and access information.

The Information Age marked the coming of the 21st Century and brought with it the ability to transfer information freely and to have instant access to knowledge that would have been difficult or impossible to find previously. The Information Age significantly impacted the economy, civilization, and social interaction.

The Biotechnology Revolution, the Sustainability Revolution, the Automation Revolution, the AI Revolution… each has brought about profound changes in the economy, creating new industries, transforming existing ones, and often redefining the way we live and work.

The prospect of hacking human motivation exceeds them all.

Humans, after all, are the common denominator in each and every revolution. Revolutionize people, and you're revolutionizing the revolutions!

If you're like most leaders, there's more than a hint of reservation as you read this. I understand the reticence. To date, most talk about culture has resonated like a pitch from a traveling elixir salesman. It's 1% common sense and 99% alcohol. Okay, not literally alcohol. Nonetheless, in lieu of tangible data they tended to rely on intoxicating language. You've probably heard about getting the right people in the right seat on the bus. Maybe you've been driving buses over twisty mountain roads for decades.

Despite the past dependence on metaphors and mystique, this is different. Failing to act in this moment will have severe consequences.

For all bus drivers, there's trouble up ahead. This intersection, where individual happiness meets work head-on, is a deadly crossroad where dreams are killed instantly and hope bleeds out amidst the wreckage. Statistically, more than two-thirds of all who journey this route will face crippling disappointment (the latest number from Gallup is 69%.) I'm not just referring to rank-and-file employees either. Board members, CEOs, and middle managers are among the casualties too. Their survival, it turns out, is directly linked to the well-being of everybody else on the bus.

Leaders are only as effective as the followers they lead. There are thousands of principles about being a leader. We've been overdue for the principles that explain what makes people follow in the first place.

What Operating System Is This?

I remember when Microsoft first launched Windows. The days of DOS (disk operating system) with its monochromatic text and alphanumeric commands were transformed into the visual experience of pointing and clicking. When a computer booted up back then, it first launched DOS, then Windows. You could literally watch the DOS boot sequence being typed out on the screen before the computer transformed itself into a drag-and-drop environment. The old operating system was still there, but Windows ran on top of it, revolutionizing everything.

Workplaces are doing something similar. The old operating system of earning a paycheck is still there. But another operating system is running on top of it, transforming work into an elaborate tactile adventure adorned with career incentives, office politics, upward mobility, and a sense of identity.

My dad grew up during the Great Depression. His parents were artists. And when the stock market collapsed in 1929, food was a struggle. One of nine family members, my dad experienced firsthand the connection between work and sustenance, between responsibility and viability. Work was part of the human biorhythm, and he took to it with a whistle and a smile.

When the Japanese bombed Pearl Harbor, my dad joined the Navy. There were days in the South Pacific when he didn't know if he'd see home again, or get married, or raise a family, or grow old someday. Experiences like that forged a mindset that came to characterize the Greatest Generation. My dad knew how to face death without giving up on life. The two concepts were somehow intrinsically linked. So were sweat and satisfaction, pain and progress, agony and ecstasy. The whole human experience was like a finely tuned ecosystem consisting of highs and lows and a code that made it all make sense in the end. People viewed themselves as part of a story with a moral and a message. They seemed to understand that the hero must fight dragons and solve riddles and scale mountains on the way to living happily ever after.

Somehow, in today's world, that story got replaced. Instead of an epic tale of adventure and meaning, the modern narrative reads more like a reality show where everybody's famous for being famous. For the first time in our nation's history the wealth of one generation is funding the coddling of the generation behind it. The incubation period for adulthood has nearly doubled, with a growing number of young men depending on financial help from their parents well into their 30s.

But for all the differences between the Greatest Generation of yesterday and the millennials of today, there's one core attribute that hasn't changed: **somewhere deep inside, people long to work.** Maybe it doesn't look like they do, but there are desires of the heart in each of us that can only be met through the exercise we call work. Every human being is born with:

- A basic instinct for agency
- An affinity for things that matter
- A desire to function within a community

For my dad's generation, these intrinsic drives were unobscured. They were on display in monumental achievements like the D-day Landing or the American space program, as well as in the ordinary, consistent routines of daily life.

Part of the problem lies with the indulgent psychology of an increasingly entitled population. But let's be honest. Companies are a big part of the problem too. And not because they coddle their people excessively. In fact, it's the opposite. The value proposition offered by most employers hasn't kept pace with the evolving needs of the workforce. As I've been explaining, just hold Maslow's Hierarchy next to each generation of workers and it's obvious how much things have changed.

The Pandemic Lens

The COVID pandemic changed things too. As it ended and the smoke cleared, the notion of getting back to normal was eventually exposed as a mere mirage. We weren't going back. For an entire generation, the three-year break from reality caused us to stop and recalibrate things. It altered the way we think about work and the already tenuous relationship between our jobs and the rest of life. We didn't leave work because we were bed-ridden by illness. The pandemic gave us permission to pause everything and reexamine things. If the whole world can just stop, then why can't I? And so we did.

"Now Hiring" became the sign of the times. Literally. The desperate pleas for someone willing to work became the soundtrack of an economy in turmoil. Restaurants, retail stores, big box chains, hotels, gas stations… everywhere you turned, companies were short staffed. Many shops reduced the hours they were open, alternating days, or shutting down completely. Even really popular brands with lines of customers were shuttering their operations simply because they didn't have the people they needed to run the business.

So where have they gone? Where are all the people who used to work the jobs that keep the world moving? They didn't all die from COVID. So where are they? The Great Resignation started when the pandemic sent people home to rethink their lives. As soon as the world stopped, it was like the workforce had been awoken from a dream. Their whole lives they'd been pressing forward numbly into the rush of everyday urgencies. But once the world stopped, they actually took a minute to think about what it all meant… to them… personally. What they saw was a life that was sailing along at cruising altitude, but in a direction they hadn't really evaluated… or had a voice in to begin with. Now wide awake, the notion of continuing on terrified them. Then, in unison, 5 million workers began walking away from their jobs. The next month it was another 5 million. This pattern would repeat itself over and over. During the three years that followed, more than 150 million people left the labor force.

Some were grabbing a brass ring and finally pursuing what they wanted instead of whatever paid the most money. Others were finally admitting how torturous their current situation had become, and even if they didn't know a better path to take, they couldn't tolerate staying on a bad one. Still others simply went home to be with their children, or to lick their wounds, or to stop and breathe.

For businesses, the whole ordeal has been crippling. Wherever manpower is needed, there's been a significant downturn in efficacy. Entire work shifts are going unfilled. The remaining employees are working double to fill in the gaps. In many places, output is a fraction of the levels it once reached. No doubt you've experienced it yourself when you've been turned away from a restaurant without enough servers, or stood in long lines at retail stores who lacked checkout clerks.

The labor crisis we're experiencing today is reminiscent of the ones that followed world wars, when entire generations of able-bodied men and women were killed or disabled. Many employers are desperate. Some have been unable to weather the storm at all.

Here's the kicker. What happened to the labor force beginning in 2020 wasn't actually caused by the pandemic. It was merely exposed by it. Truth be told, the labor force has been living in a metaphorical state of illness for decades. As I've tried to emphasize in this book, the die was cast long before today's workers were even born. Despite the shock and enigma defining conversations about our unpredictable work force, the evolution of workplace psychology shouldn't be a mystery to any of us. It's part of a predictable, scientific pattern we've known about for generations. Chances are you learned about it in school. But somehow the trees have managed to obscure our view of the forest.

Everyone wrestles with work. It's both a four-letter word describing life's unavoidable excrement and a universal expression that erupts from deep inside every living creature at one point or another. It's simultaneously a confining obligation and the very path to freedom. History has demonstrated work's misuses as well as its pertinence. Work can bring a soul to life or kill it. When work flows from autonomy, it has an invigorating effect. When work is excessively coerced, it suffocates. As Abraham

Lincoln observed, "Free labor has the inspiration of hope. Pure slavery has no hope." 150 years and 30-plus Presidents later, great companies inspire hope while coercive ones enslave, quietly cannibalizing their own flesh and bankrupting their potential.

We are living in a defining moment between those two extremes.

The connection between work and inner meaning has been talked about since the days of the ancient philosophers. Probably longer. But finding fulfilling work has been an idealistic target that very few people ever attain and most companies sidestep. Today, however, it's something you can no longer afford to ignore. Increasingly, the workforce is demanding better alignment between their personal sense of meaning and the work they do all day. Like it or not, they're looking for jobs that let them feel more connected to the natural rhythm inside them. That's what drove the Great Resignation of 2021. Competition for talent is fierce. Even if you're fortunate enough to have a staff made up of drum-pounding unicorns, you can be sure that other companies have them in their sights, looking to poach them from your ranks. You can't afford to miss a beat or they'll be gone before the chorus starts.

Happiness vs. Culture

But I must warn you, this is not a trivial undertaking. In days past, conversations about culture meant little more than slathering the workplace in a layer of emotional sucrose. But sugar highs bring a corresponding crash. A decade ago, Tony Hsieh emerged as the Willy Wonka of employee happiness. Hsieh was obsessed with its effect on human performance, a quest that turned his company, Zappos, into a business worth $1.2 billion and made him a role model for cultivating morale, engagement, and productivity. Hsieh was the pioneer of many important workplace innovations and his book, *Delivering Happiness*, was quickly regarded as the bible of vibrant culture. But his thesis of happiness – like his life – comes bookended by a sobering truth. Positivity is no mere incantation you simply pronounce over an organization. True happiness and fulfillment have complex, elusive origins. Despite his quest to infuse the work experience with joy, Hsieh's own answers land incomplete. Tragically, Hsieh devolved from a mascot for the happiness movement to its ultimate deserter, a journey detailed in Kirsten Grind and Katherine Sayre's riveting book, *Happy at Any Cost: The Revolutionary Vision and Fatal Quest of Zappos CEO Tony Hsieh*. The authors write:

> "Tony's path to the burning shed in New London, Connecticut was much more complicated and heart-breaking than we had first realized. His journey had actually started years earlier, with a fundamental goal that many people can surely relate to: he wanted to be happy. His desire to achieve happiness, and especially to spread it to those around him, was so great that he staked his entire career, and his livelihood, on that goal. It was his life's mission, and it was ultimately his downfall."

You'll have to read Grind and Sayre's book to get the whole story. But basically, Hsieh made it his life's mission to quantify happiness and personify it in the business landscape. In the end, it killed him. Since Hsieh, the pied piper of happiness, was unable to operationalize it in his own life and work, that should be a warning to us all. A happy workplace is not easily achieved. And once achieved, sustaining it can prove even more difficult.

Hsieh's efforts notwithstanding, it's clear that happiness must play a role in architecting the workplace of the future. The upside is undeniable. As someone who's been studying the science of work for most of my career, I'm more excited than ever about the untapped potential awaiting companies who can understand this moment and leverage it. In reality, the desire to work is even stronger than it was during the industrial renaissance of the 20th century. Just as companies are desperate for workers, workers are desperate to find the right opportunities to work. ***A good day's work is actually a basic human need. And when leaders understand how to offer people what they're longing to experience, it's transformational.*** Instead of the exhausting task of pushing, pleading, and coercing people to show up, they get to release the pent up longing for agency that exists in every human soul.

I first learned about these principles from sitting at the feet of some of the most influential business thinkers of our time. During my career as a ghostwriter for people whose books you've probably heard of, I spent countless hours learning from the masters of organizational effectiveness. I was privileged to work behind the scenes with everybody from Peter Drucker and John Maxwell to Ken Blanchard and Tony Robbins. I produced training courses, wrote books, and directed videos. I pored over their ideas for months on end. I had opportunities to ask questions and listen to story after story demonstrating the principles. Eventually, I found myself repeating what I'd learned for other business leaders. I coached and brainstormed. Over time, a framework emerged... and finally a system for helping companies put it all together into a culture that supports the unique objectives of the business.

I've shared some of those examples in this book. I've laid out the precepts you need to build the kind of company where people dream of spending their careers... a sought-after culture that attracts top talent and drives performance and profitability.

Singer Todd Rundgren famously belted, "I don't want to work, I just want to bang on the drum all day...." While most people are quick to appreciate the song's playful protest, let's not miss the invaluable lesson embedded in the lyric. The most valuable employees... the most dedicated and life-giving... are the ones whose zeal, consistency, and commitment create a rhythm so infectious that everyone else finds themselves naturally playing along. Sure, you might have to tell them what song to play. But once you release them into their passions, the culture takes on a life of its own.

In the future, more and more people will be looking for work that lets them bang on drums all day. They'll find it too. Savvy employers are tuned into the trend and finding ways to connect people to their passions as a means of achieving the company mission. It's the new normal. Culture is the new leadership. And it's your charge to create a culture that beats in sync with the heart of today's emerging, baffling, and absolutely essential workforce.

Reflect:
How much is culture worth at your organization?

Take the Next Step

For Every Employee Everywhere:
As you were reading this book, did it describe any of the jobs you've held throughout your career? Did you find yourself gaining new understanding of your unique needs regarding the culture where you work? Can you see how Craft, Cause & Community® have been there all along, determining whether a job is fulfilling or frustrating? You owe it to yourself to know exactly what you need from the culture around you in order to thrive. Scan the QR code below to take The Culture MRI® for yourself now. It's completely free, and you'll never be spammed. In seconds, you'll receive a personalized, detailed report based on all the key principles in this book! It might be the most important career tool you've ever used.

For C-Suite and Culture-Makers:
Culture is the new leadership! That means you need to start approaching culture like any other operational discipline. You need a way to quantify and measure it. You need a way to identify when there's a gap, and to pinpoint the exact cause. You need a way to resolve culture issues quickly and predictably... to budget for culture with a tangible ROI in mind. The days of "flavor-of-the-month" morale-boosters are gone. When it comes to culture, you can't afford to wing it. If you'd like help making your culture an operational discipline, scan this QR code:

Stop wasting money on company culture.

There are countless tips and tricks for culture. But how can you tell which ones your company needs? And engagement surveys don't give you a strategy to follow. It's time for a new solution. The Culture MRI quantifies culture so you can take specific action and measure the results.

Track Progress
Measure year-over-year improvements in performance and profitability.

Address Issues
See exactly where your culture needs attention and how to address it.

Raise Performance
Attract, retain, and engage the best of today's workforce.

Most companies see a 20%-40% gain in bottom-line performance.

www.theculturemri.com

© 2024 The Culture MRI® All Rights Reserved

www.ingramcontent.com/pod-product-compliance
Lightning Source LLC
LaVergne TN
LVHW020431070526
838199LV00025B/594/J